Bring Your Own Learning

Transform Instruction with Any Device

Lenny Schad

International Society for Technology in Education
EUGENE, OREGON · WASHINGTON, DC

Bring Your Own Learning:
Transform Instruction with Any Device
Lenny Schad

Production Editor: *Lynda Gansel*
Production Coordinator: *Emily Reed*
Development Editor: *Tracy Cozzens*
Proofreader: *Kathy Hamman*
Indexer: *Pilar Wyman*
Cover Design: *Tamra Holmes*
Book Design and Production: *Kim McGovern*

Library of Congress Cataloging-in-Publication Data
Schad, Lenny.
  Bring your own learning : transform instruction with any device / Lenny Schad.
     pages cm
  Includes index.
  ISBN 978-1-56484-338-8 (pbk. : alk. paper)
  1. Mobile communication systems in education. I. Title.
  LB1044.84.S33 2014
  371.33'4—dc23
                                                    2014000303

First Edition

ISBN: 978-1-56484-338-8 (paperback)
ISBN: 978-1-56484-488-0 (ebook)

Printed in the United States of America

Cover Art: © fotolia.com/dark_ink

ISTE® is a registered trademark of the International Society for Technology in Education.

SFI Certified Sourcing
www.sfiprogram.org
SFI-00453

About ISTE

The International Society for Technology in Education is the premier membership association for educators and education leaders committed to empowering connected learners in a connected world. Home to the ISTE Conference and Expo and the widely adopted ISTE Standards for learning, teaching, and leading in the digital age, the association represents more than 100,000 professionals worldwide.

We support our members with professional development, networking opportunities, advocacy, and ed tech resources to help advance the transformation of education. To find out more about these and other ISTE initiatives, visit iste.org.

As part of our mission, ISTE works with experienced educators to develop and publish practical resources for classroom teachers, teacher educators, and technology leaders. Every manuscript we select for publication is carefully peer reviewed and professionally edited.

Related ISTE Titles

Cell Phones in the Classroom:
A Practical Guide for Educators
Liz Kolb

Data-Driven Decision Making:
A Handbook for School Leaders
Chris O'Neal

Digital Citizenship in Schools, 2nd ed.
Mike Ribble

From Fear to Facebook:
One School's Journey
Matt Levinson

A Parent's Guide to Online Safety
Doug Fodeman & Marje Monroe

Raising a Digital Child: A Digital
Citizenship Handbook for Parents
Mike Ribble

Toys to Tools: Connecting Student
Cell Phones to Education
Liz Kolb

Safe Practices for Life Online:
A Guide for Middle and High School
Doug Fodeman & Marje Monroe

Web 2.0: How-To for Educators
Gwen Solomon & Lynne Schrum

Web 2.0: New Tools, New Schools
Gwen Solomon & Lynne Schrum

To see all books available from ISTE, please visit iste.org/bookstore.

About the Author

 For nine years, **Lenny Schad** served as the chief information officer for Katy Independent School District (KISD, Texas), a Houston-area district of 67,000 students, recognized nationally for technology innovation. Through his leadership, KISD embarked on a mobile learning initiative focusing on Web 2.0 integration, digital citizenship, and mobile devices.

Schad graduated from the University of Wyoming with a bachelor's degree in management information systems and has worked in the technology field for 25 years. During that time, his career took him into many business sectors where he established a successful leadership and management track record. His range of business experience includes hospitality, government, oil and gas, investment banking, and education. Highlights of his career include managing and leading Technology Departments for the 1991 Economic Summit of Industrialized Nations and the 1992 Republican National Convention, as well as creating and managing Technology Departments for joint ventures and global organizations. He is a recognized leader whose innovative, process-oriented management style has led to highly effective Information Technology Departments.

His recognitions include the National School Board Association's "20 to Watch" educators for 2008, the Consortium of School Networking (CoSN) Volunteer Hall of Fame, CoSN 2011 National School District Team Award, CIO Leadership Forum 2011 Next Level Leadership Award, and CoSN 2013 Withrow Chief Technology Officer (CTO) Award Honorable Mention.

In January 2013, Schad started a new role as chief information technology officer for the Houston Independent School District. One of his first tasks for the nation's sixth largest school district is implementing a 1:1 program, starting with high school students.

The opinions expressed in this book are the author's and do not necessarily reflect those of his past or current employers.

Acknowledgments

I would like to start by acknowledging the Technology Department at KISD. My leadership team there was without a doubt the sharpest group of technology professionals I have worked with over the course of my 25 years in the technology field. Their willingness to think outside the box was truly amazing and the reason why KISD has such a great reputation in the area of technology. Their dedication to maintaining the high standards expected by our stakeholders never ceased to amaze me. When you have department staff like this, it gives you much more freedom to be creative as a chief information officer. They balanced my wild ideas with a dose of reality that is absolutely necessary. The individuals in the Technology Department were the ones who made visions a reality and my job very easy; for their talents, I am so grateful.

I would like to commend KISD Superintendent Alton Frailey. Successful projects, especially ones that involve cultural change, must start at the top. Frailey's commitment to our three-year strategic plan was evident from Day One. He was visible, vocal, and supportive throughout all three years, in the goods times and bad. From my perspective, that is the definition of leadership. In that same vein, the school board needs to be acknowledged for having the vision and forethought to approve the mobile learning strategic plan and—just like Frailey—providing excellent top-down leadership and support. The board members showed the district nothing but support for this project.

I want to acknowledge the administrators, teachers, students, and parents. This was a community project, and success or failure depended on each of these groups. They pushed us, questioned us, and even fought us, yet here KISD stands, four years later, continuing the mobile journey.

Dedication

To my parents: Mom and Dad, thank you for all your support and encouragement growing up. It was your foundation that helped me become the person I am today.

To Kristie, Kelsey, and Dylan: Thank you for your love, support, and humor. You gave me encouragement and kept me grounded. I can always count on the three of you. I love you.

Contents

Contents

Contents

Contents

Introduction

If we are going to change the conversation from "Why mobile learning?" to "How do we implement mobile learning?" we need tools and road maps to drive that change. That is why I have written this book. I served as the chief information officer of the Katy Independent School District (KISD, Texas) for nine years.

At the time I wrote this book, KISD had completed Year Three of what had evolved into a mobile education strategy. We had three years' worth of experience, lessons learned, successes, failures, and data allowing for the creation of a succinct and detailed road map.

Mobile learning is such a radical change from the traditional education model that for this transformation to become mainstream, it must first be understood and then accepted by all stakeholder groups involved in the educational system—the school board, the superintendent, district staff, campus principals, teachers, and parents. Therefore, the intended audience for this book is anyone involved in that system. It doesn't matter where your education system stands now for it to undergo a mobile transformation.

School systems implementing mobile learning or bring-your-own-device (BYOD) programs can use this book as a reference or checklist, helping to:

* identify things not considered,

* provide solutions for issues, and

* avoid mistakes we made.

School systems considering mobile learning can take our road map and use it as a starting point for their implementation, adapting it to the culture and readiness level of their environment. This road map is applicable regardless of the size of a district because the issues encountered throughout implementation are universal.

My goal for this book is for district leadership teams, administrators, board members, teachers, and parents to walk away with the following key points and knowledge:

- Clear understanding of why we need to promote mobile learning

- Clear understanding of what mobile learning is and what it looks like

- Clear understanding of the steps necessary for mobile learning to be successful

- Clear understanding that implementation is an evolution and needs time to become systemic in any educational system

- Clear understanding of the benefits of mobile learning or BYOD programs

Our district, from 2009–12, saw tremendous results through the implementation of our strategic goal, beyond improved test scores. I am anxious to share those results with you and hope that mobile learning becomes mainstream for all K–12 educational institutions.

I am by no means saying this is the only way to implement a mobile education program. However, based on what we saw over those three years, I can say this book outlines a road map with proven success.

This book is divided into three parts.

- The chapters in Part One frame the mobile learning foundation and provide background information leading up to the development of our three-year strategic plan.

- The chapters in Part Two provide a year-by-year overview of each strategic initiative.

- The chapters in Part Three present my closing thoughts related to the KISD three-year mobile program and discuss the next steps for the district.

Many documents and forms related to KISD's mobile learning implementation can be found under the Resources tab at my website, www.LennyJSchad.com.

PART ONE

Framing the Mobile Learning Foundation

Mobile learning is a radical change from the traditional education model. It will transform your school system in ways far beyond simply allowing mobile devices into your classrooms. The implementation process will be unique for each school system because at its core this transformation is all about changing the culture.

This book is applicable to any educational system regardless of where it stands in this transformation. It strives to put into context these considerations:

- Why a school system should change to a mobile learning model

- How the mobile learning model started

- How to plan for the transition to mobile learning

The chapters in Part One build on each other to provide you with an understanding of how KISD addressed each of these areas and should help you establish a clear foundation for mobile learning.

CHAPTER 1

It's Not If, It's When

It's time to start changing the focus of our conversations related to mobile learning from theory or concepts to implementation strategies.

As our district's chief information officer, responsible for all district technology as well as instructional technology, I participated in many panels and gave numerous webinars and presentations devoted to mobile learning or "bring your own device" (BYOD) programs. From 2009–12 , most of the questions from participants stayed the same, focusing on two key areas: mobile learning concepts and barriers to implementation.

I spent very little time talking about implementation-related strategies or steps. At a recent education conference, I was on a mobile learning panel and was asked this as my final question: "Next year at this time, what are you hoping the conversation regarding mobile learning will look like?"

My response was simple: "I want the conversation to be focused on implementation strategies and steps, *not* mobile learning theory." Let me explain why I believe we are ready to move from theory to implementation.

Three recent leading indicators have provided data supporting the transition from theory to implementation. These three indicators are research, resources, and implementations.

Research

The New Media Consortium's yearly *Horizon Report* (www.nmc.org/horizon-project) lists the emerging technologies likely to have significant effects on education and a time frame its advisory board anticipates for widespread adoption. The *2009 Horizon Report: K–12 Edition* listed mobiles as one of the technologies to watch with an adoption time frame of two to three years.

Use of mobiles was picking up steam as smartphone technologies became mainstream. The functionality of these devices had moved beyond phone and text to having the ability to connect to Wi-Fi networks, provide GPS functionality, and run applications. However, even though the power of the smartphone and its expanded functionality was gaining recognition in the private sector and higher education, most K–12 systems didn't even consider incorporating mobile devices into learning.

Mobiles, particularly cell phones, were still predominately banned in K–12 schools and were widely viewed as inhibitors to education rather than enablers. For those few K–12 systems looking into the potential of mobile devices, educators were uncertain how the functionality of these devices could be incorporated into classrooms. Beyond the negative stigma mobile devices had in the K–12 space, one of the biggest issues in 2009 was availability of educational resources capable of operating on these mobile devices. As a result, the power of smartphones was changing the landscape for the private sector and higher education, but not affecting K–12 classrooms.

The *2010 Horizon Report: K–12 Edition* again listed mobile devices as a technology to watch, but with a one-year or less mainstream adoption window. The depth and breath of mobile device use continued to expand in 2010, extending to users younger than those in 2009.

We also saw the introduction of tablet devices, which provide a middle ground between the smartphone and laptop. Tablets offer the same functionality, feature sets, and applications as smartphones, but with bigger displays. The continued need for users to have more and more information and functionality anytime, anywhere was driving market penetration.

However, while the number and age ranges of users were on the rise, very little had changed when it came to K–12 educators' perceptions of these devices in the classroom. The mobile device was still predominantly banned from all K–12 buildings, and there still was not a clear understanding of exactly how to integrate these devices into the classroom.

Barriers

The good news was that more conversations took place in K–12 education about mobile devices and their potential impacts and roles in the classroom. During those early conversations, many barriers to implementation were identified, especially existing philosophical paradigms that did not recognize the value or impact these devices could have on education. Also, policy issues and basic cultural readiness concerns needed to be addressed before districts could introduce mobile devices as educational tools. A lot of work remained beyond just device functionality, inhibiting device adoption in classrooms. None of these organizational issues were insurmountable, but they would take time to overcome.

In 2010, a few K–12 school systems, including KISD, were going beyond ideas and concepts and dipping their toes into implementation. Those of us using mobile devices in the classroom were getting lots of attention. The attention came from education stakeholder groups, such as researchers, administrators, vendors, and school board members from all over the country. The conversations were focused on organizational barriers and how we were addressing them.

In most cases when we were contacted by a school system, we spoke with one individual who was trying to figure out how to introduce the concept of mobile learning to the whole system. Rarely were the conversations with a leadership team ready to begin the mobile journey. Even though the *2010 Horizon Report: K–12 Edition* had the expectation of one year or less for mainstream adoption, I just didn't feel the philosophical change was occurring with enough breadth and depth in the K–12 space to see such a radical change in less than a year. The good news for 2010 was that some districts were implementing mobile devices in the classroom, and conversations about mobile possibilities in the K–12 space were starting to occur on a broader scale.

Cloud Computing

The *2011 Horizon Report: K–12 Edition* again listed mobile devices as a technology to watch with a one-year or less time frame for mainstream adoption. It also listed cloud computing as a technology to watch with an adoption time frame of one year or less. I believe industry experts were now making the connection between these two technologies. The power of mobile devices, whether smartphones or tablets, is their ability to have access anytime, anywhere. The real question—and one of the main barriers for mobiles in the K–12 space—was access anytime, anywhere *to what?* That is where cloud computing became a significant player when discussing mobiles.

Cloud computing began providing answers to the question of *access to what* for the K–12 space. The introduction and integration of cloud solutions—particularly those solutions that teachers and students could leverage—created the value proposition for mobiles in the classroom. Now mobiles had relevance for K–12 education.

I don't believe that mobiles are a year or less away from mainstream adoption, as predicted by the *Horizon Report;* rather, I believe a two- to three-year adoption period is more realistic. My reason is simple. The majority of conversations related to mobile learning are still at the "Do we or don't we?" philosophical level. If mobiles are going to go mainstream in the K–12 space, the conversation must be "How do we?"

The "Learning on-the-Go" Grants

Other sources of reserach data supporting my assertion that we are ready to move from theory to implementation are preliminary reports from programs supported by the U.S. Federal Communications Commission's (FCC's) "Learning on-the-Go" pilot program. These grants, created and awarded for the 2011–12 school year and funded from E-Rate funds, focused on obtaining verifiable data showing mobile learning's impact on K–12 education.

To gather as much data from participating school systems as possible, the FCC waived stipulations regarding where the devices can be used. Current E-Rate policy mandates that E-Rate money can be used to pay for any data plan service fees as long as the devices are used on school premises. For recipients of these grants, that policy was waived, allowing students to take the devices home and still receive E-Rate funds for the data plan.

Twenty school systems were awarded these grants. KISD was one of the chosen schools and the only one in Texas. Recipients had to track various data points throughout the school year and provide preliminary and final results specifically targeted in the grant application. The recipient school systems were categorized into two groups: those that had implemented mobile learning (KISD was in this group) and those that would implement mobile learning if awarded the grant. Most recipients were school systems wanting to implement some type of mobile learning program and in need of funding. A few of the recipients, like KISD, had already implemented some type of mobile program and were going to use the grant funding to offset current expenditures or expand an already-existing program. KISD used the grant money in the third year of our strategic plan to expand the mobile device program to additional campuses.

Preliminary reports from the grant schools were submitted in February 2012. I had the opportunity to review a number of these reports, and the results were outstanding, mirroring results seen in KISD. Our issues and concerns were similar to those of other school systems using mobile learning. The hope of all recipients and, quite honestly, all schools capable of receiving E-Rate money is that the

FCC will see the value of mobile learning to K–12 education and change current policies, allowing funding to occur regardless of device use at school or home.

If further research supports these preliminary results, the value and impact of mobile learning to K–12 education will be hard to dispute. Whether or not this research is sufficient to change policies is uncertain—only time will tell. However, should there be a change in the current E-Rate policies related to student use and location, the number of implementations will quickly increase.

Resources

Another area that supports the transition from theory to implementation is the growing availability of educational resources. When KISD began its journey into mobile learning in 2009, one of our major constraints was the limited availability of educational resources capable of operating on a mobile device. Of course, devices provided access to the Internet for research. Teachers were using QR codes (barcodes) in their material to link students to websites they wanted students to research. Web 2.0 tools, such as blogs and wikis, were used and very adaptable to mobile devices. We used applications like Sketchy, which provided students the opportunity to animate homework assignments—for example, with an illustration of the precipitation cycle.

Plus, our classrooms used the built-in functions of the mobile devices, such as the camera and video. While streaming video was common in traditional classroom settings, the educational vendors had not adapted many of their videos for mobile devices. As a result, the number of videos available for our mobile devices was limited. Additionally, KISD's internal wireless network experienced some bandwidth issues when multiple classrooms were using streaming video. Although limited in availability, streaming video was a powerful and frequently used instructional tool.

These were the only mobile resources available in 2009. Even though these tools provided significant learning opportunities and growth beyond the traditional paper and pencil, we needed more resources capable of functioning on mobile devices. We began reaching out to the major educational vendors, asking them not only to develop mobile-enabled applications, but, more important, to begin the process of porting over their traditional desktop-based suite of products to a mobile environment.

Vendors Recognize Mobile Learning

In 2010, a number of new vendors entered the education marketplace with products capable of embracing a mobile learning environment. Also, some of the major educational vendors transitioned their desktop-based applications to mobile devices.

In 2010 we began using applications that provided interactive manipulation for science and math homework. For example, students in science class learning about electronic circuitry used software that enabled them to put the various elements of a circuit together manually on their screens. If they put the elements of the circuit together correctly, the light bulb on their device would turn on, and if they didn't put the elements together correctly, the light would not come on. This type of interactive learning provided engagement and understanding far beyond traditional paper and pencil methods.

We also began using mobile games for learning, particularly in the math arena. This type of learning combines personal interaction with the appeal of gaming while educating the students. From the students' perspectives, they were simply playing games and having fun; what students didn't know was that they were also learning and practicing various math concepts. This type of learning allowed students to obtain higher levels of understanding.

We also saw the introduction of classroom clicker functionality via the mobile devices. This type of functionality allowed teachers to quickly assess their students' comprehension of a particular topic.

Teachers could create assessments, and each student would respond via their mobile device, providing immediate feedback to the teacher on the students' level of understanding. This type of real-time assessment allowed teachers to reteach a concept or to assess an individual student's comprehension within the classroom period. The device also had applications capable of polling, once again allowing feedback and interaction in a new and immediate fashion.

We also began seeing mobile device use expand beyond the core subjects. For example, applications were being used that made each mobile device a musical instrument. This changed the dynamics of a traditional music classroom.

Looking back over the past three years, we have seen an exponential growth of educational resources taking advantage of the feature sets inherent to mobile devices. Throughout the course of our implementation, we solicited teacher feedback multiple times during each school year. This feedback provided teachers with an avenue to voice their successes, areas of concern, and any barriers they felt were preventing the adoption of mobile devices in their classrooms. When I compare teacher feedback from 2009 to 2012, availability of resources—once considered the top barrier to adoption—is no longer mentioned. Although not a barrier to adoption, availability of mobile education resources lags significantly behind traditional computer-based resources. This is an area that must become a high priority for every educational vendor.

Cloud-Based School Systems

Although educational vendors certainly are major players in the area of educational resources, school systems themselves have a responsibility as well. KISD worked hard to migrate as many of what were once internal resources to the cloud and continues to do so.

When I refer to internal resources, I am talking about any educational resource requiring authentication into our internal network. By migrating as many of our resources as possible to the cloud, anytime, anywhere access is possible, providing the user has Internet connectivity. Additionally, when a new software package is evaluated by KISD, it must meet the nonnegotiable requirement that the application be web-enabled and make use of cloud functionality. This standard requirement for software supports the desire for making any educational resource used by the students of our district available anytime, anywhere.

Implementations

Mobile learning has picked up speed since 2009. Discussions pertaining to mobile learning became mainstream, especially during the 2011–12 school year. Even though the conversations still focus on "if," all you have to do is look at any conference or webinar agenda or pick up any educational trade magazine, and you will see that mobile learning or BYOD dominates the list of sessions or articles.

The number of school systems investigating or actually implementing mobile programs has grown significantly. This supports the move from "Is this real?" to "Yes, it's real, and it's transformational."

During the 2011 school year, I experienced a dramatic increase in the number of inquiries into the mobile learning world. The exciting thing for me was that the majority of inquiries were from leadership teams or superintendents ready to tackle the mobile learning challenge. I talked with board members from other school systems, helping them understand the concept of mobile learning and the challenges associated with its implementation. I also had a number of conversations related to BYOD.

I heard a lot of comparisons made between mobile learning and BYOD, showing that many people think that they are one and the same. This is not the case.

Mobile learning is an educational strategy focusing on instructional approaches and cultivating a philosophical change in instruction. Effective mobile learning requires a fundamental change in how teachers deliver instruction, away from the traditional paper-and-pencil model. The success of mobile learning is not based solely on the devices used in the classroom. It depends on teaching methods that incorporate the devices into the process of learning. (See Chapter 3 for a discussion of this philosophical change.)

BYOD, on the other hand, enables a personal device owned by the student to become a tool that helps accomplish the mobile learning strategy. BYOD is about the device and how a school district chooses to allow access and manage its use. BYOD by itself will have no impact on student achievement or engagement if the instruction is still based on the traditional paper-and-pencil model. Rather, BYOD must be an element of a higher strategic goal of fundamentally changing how teachers deliver instruction. I will go into further detail about BYOD strategies in Chapter 8.

As a result of this confusion regarding mobile learning and BYOD, I make sure in all my presentations, webinars, and panels that I clearly articulate this fundamental difference between the two.

I believe now is the time for the K–12 environment to transition to mobile learning. If we want students capable of competing in a global market, we must incorporate the tools that will be used in a global market. I hope that, in the coming years, we will see a continued increase in the number of schools that embrace mobile learning.

CHAPTER 2

How My Mobile Vision Began

My journey into mobile learning started in 2008 and centered around two events: a conference I attended that explored mobile devices and cloud-based solutions and my simple investigation into what my own children and their friends were doing with their technology devices.

The Convergence of Mobility and Cloud-Based Solutions

The event that gave me my first glimpse into the possibilities of mobile learning was a two-day Microsoft Public Sector conference focusing on mobility and cloud-based solutions.

At this conference, *mobility* focused specifically on enabling the workforce to access information pertinent to their work processes anytime, anywhere. At the core of this concept were mobile devices and the facts that these devices needed constant connectivity to the Internet and access to applications outside the traditional business network.

The major focus was on cellular devices with discussions and presentations targeted at two specific areas in the cellular market. The first area was the change in the functional paradigm regarding the perceived use of these mobile devices from simply communication tools to productivity devices on which actual work could be accomplished. The second area comprised trends and predictions for the mobile market, including market growth, device evolution, and application and functionality evolution.

Cloud solution presentations focused on the costs and benefits of moving to the cloud. Discussions helped the audience frame the return on investment (ROI) model, outlining the considerations and factors making up the ROI calculation. Also discussed were what services and functions could be moved to the cloud.

At this event, I started to understand at a deeper level how mobile devices—with their ability to access cloud-based solutions anytime, anywhere—were going to be a game changer. Mobility and cloud-based solutions meant actual universal access to resources and information without being tethered to an organizational network or device. The organizations considered were from private and public sectors, including higher education. Interestingly, K–12 education wasn't discussed. I wondered, why couldn't this be a game changer for K–12? Although the presentations and discussions focused on the business side of operations, I could easily correlate each discussion to an educational setting. On a philosophical level, the idea of teachers and students using mobile devices to access instructional resources made a lot of sense; however, I found a lot of gaps as I started to apply this idea to a real K–12 education system.

The cloud-based solutions discussed were from an infrastructure standpoint (such as file server, storage, application, and email), which were relevant to everyone in the public and private sectors. But how many cloud-based instructional resources or teacher/student collaboration tools had been developed? A game changer for education in KISD would be providing anytime, anywhere access to resources, such as instructional content, instructional tools, information, and educational applications to all of our stakeholder groups. The problem was that access to these various resources was limited to district devices accessing our internal private network or to a specific group of district employees via some type of remote-access software package. Not exactly a game changer because most organizations had remote capabilities already, and it didn't accomplish the anytime, anywhere concept for stakeholder groups beyond a select few employees. The power of mobile devices and cloud computing was extending the boundaries of our internal resources and not limiting the devices that could access them. It was then that I began to formulate my concept of mobile learning.

If we could put instructional resources out into the cloud—allow students to store their files in the cloud, get their email, and, most important, do their homework with tools in the cloud—we would have the foundational layer in place allowing for anytime, anywhere education.

I remember coming back from the conference and attending the superintendent's cabinet meeting Monday morning. Of course, the first question asked was how was the conference? I remember my response to this day. I told the cabinet, based on what I was exposed to at Microsoft, the next five to seven years would be the most transformational years K–12 education has seen in decades. Mobility and cloud-based solutions would transform and redefine the traditional classroom and class-day paradigms.

In my opinion, this transformation wasn't an option. As a K–12 school system, we had two choices. We could blaze this transformational path, or we could wait for the trail to be established and follow. Now, the problem I had with waiting for the trail to be established was that we would forever be behind. In some instances this is absolutely the right decision. However, in this particular case, I didn't want to wait, and KISD chose the trailblazer path.

Those educational institutions embracing and implementing this new philosophy, I felt, would have a huge educational advantage when it came to preparing their students for life in the digital world. This educational advantage would create competition among the various K–12 institutions. Parents who had the option would move their children to those institutions providing this new way of educating. The main point here is that mobility and cloud-based solutions had the potential to change the school day, the learning opportunities, and support infrastructure available for teachers, students, and parents. We in K–12 education could not ignore this opportunity. To do so would be an injustice to our students, who will live the rest of their lives in this new digital world.

Students Are Already Connected

When I was considering a mobile learning strategy, I realized the benefits of implementing cloud-based resources were predicated on anytime, anywhere access from some type of untethered device. As I struggled with the device piece of the puzzle, the answer started to emerge by simple observation—watching my own children and talking with their friends.

In 2008, my daughter was a senior in high school, and my son was a freshman in high school. After I came home from the Microsoft conference, I began to watch my kids, observing how, what, and why they used a certain type of technology device. We have all heard and seen fun facts about digital natives, so I won't rehash their working parameters. The fact that you are reading this book tells me you have a good grasp of who they are and what they are looking for. It was interesting, though, watching my children doing homework. The only technology devices they had were cell phones and laptop/desktops. The most frequently used device during the homework cycle was the cell phone. Now, I am not foolish enough to believe the activity occurring on the cell phones was all about the school work, but when my children were working, texting and accessing information online were major components of how they were completing assignments. These devices provide opportunities for the children to collaborate and to verify and seek out information.

The laptop was used, too, but only as the device to type on and maybe access the Internet to do some research. I started to pay closer attention to how and for what purpose the cell phones were being used beyond talking or texting, not isolated specifically to education. I discovered the devices were being used to access the Internet, update social networking sites, collaborate, email (rarely), take pictures, research, and create videos, among many other uses. Now, how many of those things that I just mentioned could be used in a classroom setting? The really interesting thing was, given the choice and availability of their cell phones or laptops in their social lives, my children unanimously chose their cell phones.

It was at this point I wanted to go beyond the walls of the happy Schad family and see how the devices were being used with a broader audience. I began to watch kids' use of technology devices when we were at social events, the movies, dinner, or any other gathering. My own children's cell phone use was consistent with what I observed with other children their age.I concluded that cell phones were devices most secondary-age children had. They were their constant connection anytime, anywhere to resources that interested them in their private lives.

My mobile vision was becoming clearer. However, I still had some unanswered questions. First, at the secondary level how many students, regardless of their socioeconomic status, had cell phones? And, most important, how many had cell phones with a data plan capable of accessing the Internet? I posed that question to my good friend Joe Kelly, who had been a high school principal and at that time was an area superintendent for KISD. His gut feeling prior to going out and actually polling the students was very few. "The majority have phones, but very few will have data plans providing access to the Internet," he told me. To find out, we went to some of the most economically disadvantaged junior and senior high schools in the district and asked students two simple questions: How many of you have cell phones? How many of you have data plans to access the Internet?

An overwhelming majority of students had cell phones, and surprisingly, the majority of those with cell phones had a data plan capable of accessing the Internet. The number of students with devices that had data plans was high enough for us to conclude that data-plan access was not going to be a limiting factor when considering mobile devices. This information was powerful and helped support our assumption that cell phones (at least among secondary students) were the one device that could provide anytime, anywhere access. The question still remained: Connectivity to what?

What a Mobile Vision Looks Like

At this point, I started focusing on what a mobile learning vision would look like for KISD. I knew mobile devices and cloud computing needed to have a place in K–12 education. I knew the majority of secondary students, regardless of their socioeconomic status, had mobile devices with data plans capable of accessing the Internet. I didn't know what educational resources mobile devices would access via cloud technology. I didn't know how mobile learning could be extended to the elementary level. I didn't know how this radical change in the traditional education model would be introduced, understood, and crucially, accepted. So the next step in finalizing my mobile vision was to begin analyzing and trying to address my list of "I don't know" questions.

First on my list was discovering what educational resources are required to enable mobile learning for K–12. As I began analyzing the list of existing resources used in KISD, I found that 90 percent of them were restricted to users on our internal network and were based on the traditional educational model. I knew that for mobile learning to occur, we needed to begin implementing educational resources that were engaging to students and, most important, accessible anytime, anywhere.

Using Web 2.0

I went back to what I'd observed with students using their devices. What tools were they using? One answer was Web 2.0 tools. As I began looking into these tools, I quickly discovered thousands that had educational value. These Web 2.0 tools were independent from an internal private network, only requiring access to the Internet. That was one question answered: Incorporating Web 2.0 tools would provide access to educational resources anytime, anywhere.

Stakeholder Buy-in and Digital Citizenship

The next unanswered question was how to introduce mobile learning in a way that would foster understanding and gain acceptance of our strategic goal and initiatives from our stakeholder groups. Changing the traditional educational model was not going to be easy, particularly when we started introducing Web 2.0 tools into the process. We recognized that it would entail much more than simply explaining mobile learning. We would need a focused effort that helped our stakeholders along the change process to our new educational model. The answer is that we would have to educate our stakeholders on the big picture of digital citizenship—what it means to be a digital citizen, what the digital world looks like for our students, and what tools were out there that made mobile learning possible.

We also had to communicate what KISD was doing to prepare its students to function responsibly in a digital world. Stakeholders had to understand that the changes we were making to the traditional education model by incorporating mobile learning would help our student population understand what it meant to function and live in this new digital world. For example, over the last couple of years, I had grown increasingly frustrated with our approach to Internet filtering. Now, I am not saying we should abandon Internet filtering completely, but for seven hours a day while they are in our schools, students are wrapped in a tight protective cocoon, where we control where they go, what they do, and what they see on the Internet. Then the school day ends, and for 17 hours they are in the wide open world of the Internet. What were we doing as a school system to help them operate responsibly for those 17 hours? Stakeholders needed to understand the gap between the protective cocoon students encountered at school and the unprotected digital landscape that existed beyond school filters. As a school system, we needed to figure out how to bridge that gap.

At this point, my definition of mobile learning became clear. When I first started thinking about mobile learning and the possibilities for K–12, I was focused primarily on the device and how the device would change the landscape. Once I began answering the "I don't know" questions, I came to realize that mobile learning was absolutely not about the device. It was about providing the educational resources and modes of instruction that would enable the mobile device to be a tool in that process. Changing instructional techniques was at the core of my mobile vision and would be the springboard to changing the traditional education model. Equally important in a mobile learning program was incorporating digital citizenship. Getting stakeholders to understand what it meant for our students to be successful and responsible digital citizens in the digital world, now and in the future, provided the mechanism to gain their understanding and acceptance of our strategic goal and initiatives. If KISD were to be successful with the introduction of a mobile vision, we needed to spend time with our stakeholder groups.

So, my mobile vision for KISD would encompass three areas:

Mobility. Providing anytime, anywhere access to information via district-provided or student-owned devices

Web 2.0. Having instructional resources accessible via the cloud, accommodating anytime, anywhere access

Digital citizenship. Gaining acceptance of the mobile learning model by fostering stakeholder understanding of what it means for students to be digital citizens, what their digital world looks like, and what digital tools they will be using to learn

With my vision formulated, the next step was actually getting support from the cabinet and school board to begin defining an implementation strategy. You know the old saying: timing is everything. Well, the stars had aligned, and the process of moving from vision to implementation strategy was about to hit KISD smack in the face.

CHAPTER 3

Moving from Vision to Goal

In the fall of 2009, the KISD superintendent's cabinet began discussions to identify strategic objectives our district would focus on for the upcoming 2009–10 school year. When looking at the academic challenges facing the district, the cabinet raised a number of issues and concerns. As we began to evaluate each issue or concern, a common thread emerged—student engagement. It is important to note that KISD was already academically successful. We were a recognized school district with an outstanding track record of student achievement.

During those same planning discussions, we all voiced our concerns about a growing trend we were seeing among our key stakeholders. Despite the great results and ratings KISD was achieving, our key stakeholders—administrators, teachers, students, and parents—were frustrated. We spent time talking with each of the stakeholder groups to better understand the cause of their frustration. The following sections present a summary of the input gathered from each group.

Principals

Principals were frustrated, particularly at the secondary level, by having to watch their students "power down" every day when they entered the school facilities. My colleague, Joe Kelley, vividly recalls as a high school principal watching the students coming into the building each morning and seeing how their body language and attitude would change, turning off their engagement as they powered down their personal devices. How can we expect the students to be engaged with learning when we don't allow learning to occur in a way that is relevant to them and with tools they're growing up with?

The concept seems so easy, yet K–12 education to this day still struggles with a solution. I heard an analogy once, and it was so applicable to KISD at that time. Public education is very similar to the airline industry—when children come to school, we tell them to sit down, turn off all electrical equipment, and enjoy their day.

Principals realized the devices were not simply toys in their students' lives. The mobile devices and their functionality were critical cogs in their daily functions, and we were not recognizing or appreciating their importance. Principals at every grade level were trying to provide leadership to their teachers on practices and principles that would result in greater achievement, all the while knowing these practices were not going to have a long-term effect or impact because they were not engaging the students. Teachers were pushing back, asking for more resources, tools, and support to help aid their efforts to improve engagement. Principals were getting good ideas from their teachers that would greatly improve engagement, only to run into implementation roadblocks either from a policy or technology perspective. Principals were frustrated by their inability to make needed changes.

Teachers

Teachers at all levels were frustrated because they were constantly struggling with engagement. They were striving to promote higher level thinking and 21st-century skills, but their instruction was limited by tools, systems, and practices from the traditional education model, none of which were reaching students. Teachers were studying how children of today function and learn differently. They were introduced to the "digital learner" and what their expectations were for a learning environment, only to go back into their classrooms and have almost the same resources and instructional tools my teachers had when I was in school. As a result, engagement was suffering, and frustration was mounting. They were doing their very best and trying to be as creative as possible with what they had, but their efforts were not meeting students' needs.

Frustration continued to grow the more we discussed digital learners and what and how they wanted to learn. Teachers got it; they just didn't have the tools necessary to deliver. When they tried to think outside the box, many times they were cut off because of policy concerns, technology issues, or leadership unwilling to take risks. The more we talked about what students needed, the more we heard teachers asking for help.

Parents

Parents were frustrated because they didn't see their children as digital learners and didn't understand how this new learning style affected the overall educational experience for their children. Many were afraid, misinformed, or just blind to the digital world in which their children lived. For parents, the Internet was a black hole that provided very little educational value beyond Wikipedia (I will talk about that later) and had more negative connotations than positive when it related their children. In light of the negative press the Internet was getting, most parents had no idea what their children did on computers or how to understand and guide their children in the digital world. The digital divide occurring in households was increasing with each passing year.

Parents were not seeing mobile devices, whether they were laptops or cell phones, as anything more than toys or tools (once in a while). They did not understand that the devices and the Internet were foundational cornerstones of how their children functioned on a daily basis and would remain cornerstones of how they would function for the forseeable future.

So, as parents applied their mental model of what a student should do and how a student should act to their own child's behavior, the disconnect was precipitating generational warfare. Children didn't understand the mental model parents were trying to enforce because it was so foreign and one they could not even grasp. The days of sitting quietly at a desk with no distractions were gone—that was not how children operated, and yet that was the only model parents had to draw on. Parents wanted to be involved and provide that educational foundation we all know is so important, yet they simply didn't understand how much the educational world had changed and would continue to change since their own days in the classroom.

Students

Students were probably the most frustrated group of stakeholders. They felt like they were being forced to live and learn in a time warp. The world they were growing up in was changing by the minute, and yet when they entered a school building, it was like going back in time. They were not able to articulate with great success how they learned. They knew they were far ahead of us in terms of their use of technology and its role in their lives.

To students, it was painfully obvious that we adults didn't understand the digital world they were growing up in and the importance of technology. Their classmates and friends were the only group they could relate to. As a result, outside the school day students were applying their learning styles with the tools available, creating work, and learning their way. Because they had the ability to communicate with their peers anytime, anywhere, collaboration was at the forefront in their lives outside school and a critical piece of how they learned and operated.

Although collaboration was critical to how students lived and ultimately were doing their schoolwork, they knew it would be frowned upon, so it was kept hidden, another point of frustration for students. Now, when I talk about collaboration in the fashion discussed above, in the context of students doing schoolwork, most adults immediately jump to the copying or cheating model. Yet that's not what the students were doing. They were collaborating and learning from each other. They were using their peers' individual strengths to benefit each other. When you think about it, isn't that a form of differentiated learning? School systems have been spending a lot of time talking about how best to achieve differentiated learning, and yet our students on their own were already tapping into this approach.

Consider this same concept at youth athletic events. I remember growing up and spending entire Saturdays playing football or baseball or basketball and never having the fights or arguments about who is starting, who is playing, what they are playing, are they getting the ball, etcetera. We as very young children worked it out, and everyone for the most part enjoyed the day and time spent playing, whatever sport it was. Insert adults into the mix and all hell breaks loose. All those questions I asked above became central, not only with the parents but with the children as well. My point here is this—whether in education or in organized youth activities, parents need to take a page from how children live and operate and apply what the children themselves are doing.

The Internet provides a multitude of learning opportunities and tools. In spite of the limitations of a typical classroom, we learned that today's students were adapting and using the tools, practices, and options available to them outside the normal school setting to learn their way. The frustration for them was, "Why can't this happen at school? Why must I endure a boring day with none of my tools or resources?"

Putting It Together

I wasn't surprised to discover that the information provided by our various stakeholders supported my vision for mobile learning. Each stakeholder group's concerns, or issues as they related to student engagement would in some form or fashion be addressed by the mobile learning areas of focus. This was the opening I needed to begin conversations with the superintendent's cabinet.

Now that the cabinet members had talked with each group, it was time to evaluate their feedback. While student engagement was easy to identify as an issue, solving this problem proved to be much harder than expected. Our primary challenge was overcoming our traditional mindset. This mindset was grounded in the traditional educational model that had become institutionalized within the classrooms at KISD, and we struggled to think outside of those traditional parameters. As we began looking at solutions, we evaluated a number of options.

Evaluating Support Systems and Tools

First, we started with our support systems and tools. While there were some recommendations for changes in our support systems, none of the changes would address student engagement. It was a valid area to look at, and we did get some great ideas for systemic changes. But these didn't solve our immediate problem.

When we evaluated the tools within our classrooms, we broke the tools into two categories: hardware and software. We determined that the hardware tools, such as interactive whiteboards and mobile labs, were adequate. The issue with hardware tools was professional development and simply getting the teachers to incorporate these tools into the learning process more effectively—certainly something to consider that could affect student engagement.

We also evaluated our technology infrastructure to see if there were any glaring deficiencies preventing teachers from doing what they needed in the classroom. The technical infrastructure was sound and could easily be modified to address any capacity issues that might arise from expanded use.

When we began looking into the software tools, some real opportunities came to the forefront. The tools at teachers' disposal were, for the most part, based on the traditional model and not meeting students' needs.

The software tools analysis was my foot in the door to begin the conversation about my mobile learning vision. I used the stakeholder feedback and tied it back to one of the three areas of my mobile vision.

The cabinet's immediate reaction was to jump right back to the traditional model and come up with reasons why it would work. Each time the traditional model was shown to be a barrier, I would refer back to the stakeholder feedback. What we were doing was not working. We had to think outside the box. It took a lot of conversations with the cabinet, but the members ultimately came to the same conclusion I did. KISD needed to change instruction. Engagement was not about hardware, software, or mobile devices; it was about the instruction being delivered inside classrooms.

The Strategic Goal: Changing How Teachers Teach

Our path forward had become clear: our strategic goal was to change instruction philosophically. That's it; we found the key! We needed to change how teachers were instructing in the classroom. How hard could that be?

As we began discussions around our newly defined goal and how we would implement this philosophical change using my mobile vision, it became apparent just how set in stone the traditional model of educating students had become and just how difficult it would be to change.

I have been in education since 2003, and one of the many things I have learned moving from the private sector to public education is how averse to change these systems really are. I also understand why they are so adverse to change. Change in any form—whether cultural, systemic, or procedural—takes time, understanding, and an implementation pace acceptable to those being affected. Typically, at least one of those keys to implementing change breaks down, causing the change effort either to fail or struggle for adoption. From a teacher's perspective, when issues interrupt the educational class period, the teacher never gets that time back, putting him or her behind the eight ball to make up for lost time—with an instructional and testing calendar looming in the background.

In KISD, we had fostered a culture of change over the five years leading up to the time that the mobile learning discussions occurred. I learned what can hinder change the hard way in my first two years with the district. I did not have a real understanding of or appreciation for the culture of education and the inherent differences between public education and the private sector. Those first two years saw the implementation of a new student management system, a new gradebook system, and implementation of locked down desktops, standardization of software, and a new curriculum management system. All of this was necessary and benefited the district tremendously in the long term. However, it was too much too fast. As a result, my first two years were very difficult.

Years three, four, and five were also filled with systemic and technical changes, but with a much better implementation cycle. Pacing, readiness, support, and professional development were given attention and were cornerstones to each subsequent initiative's success.

Even though my first two years were rocky, our team did not back away from the cultural reality of change. Each year as the school year closed, we distributed a district-wide email, highlighting to everyone the tech changes that would occur over the summer and what employees could expect when school started the following year. This culture of change is important to any organization. Change is a reality that must be part of every strategy for long-term success, regardless of whether the organization is private or public.

So, during the 2009–10 discussions, we already had the cultural expectation for change. We needed to identify what would best foster and enable a philosophical change to instruction.

We started by again reviewing the feedback from our stakeholders. We applied that feedback to my mobile vision, only this time through the lens of changing instruction.

Principals talked about the disengagement caused by powering down, so we needed to look at devices and how to incorporate them into the classroom.

Teachers talked about not having the resources pertinent to digital learners, so we needed to look at educational resources and the Web2.0 tools that would be made available in the classroom.

Parents struggled with understanding the digital world and how it changes education, so we needed to formulate a digital citizenship program.

Our students wanted all of the above.

When we solved for the problem of changing instruction based on the feedback, it didn't take long for us to arrive at the same three key initiatives I had defined in my mobile vision. We would introduce Web 2.0 tools into the arsenal of resources available to teachers. We would initially dip our toes into the mobile world by providing some type of device to a subset of our student population, ultimately planning for a fourth initiative—districtwide bring-your-own-device (BYOD) implementation. Throughout these initiatives, we would focus on digital citizenship. We knew that changing instruction would be a difficult concept for all stakeholders. As a result, we knew a dedicated focus was required that allowed our stakeholders the ability first to understand, then accept, and ultimately support our plan.

The strategic initiatives we felt would accomplish our strategic goal of changing how teachers teach were:

- Web 2.0 integration
- mobile learning
- digital citizenship
- bring your own device (BYOD)

The next task was to rough out an implementation cycle we felt would allow for proper pacing and understanding, while not completely throwing the district's primary objective of increasing student engagement into a tailspin.

We knew this was something that couldn't be implemented quickly; we need to crawl before we walked before we sprinted. We would need measurable criteria to evaluate the following:

- Was instruction being delivered differently?

- Was the change in instruction affecting learning positively or negatively?

- Was the change of instruction achieving our primary goal of improving student engagement?

- Did stakeholder groups understand and accept this change?

We defined a three-year implementation plan, to be reviewed yearly, that we felt would absolutely facilitate the philosophical change to instruction. That plan with its initiatives described looked like this:

2009–10

Web 2.0 Integration: Introduce Web 2.0 tools to teachers at every campus.

Mobile Learning: Pilot mobile learning with one grade level at one campus.

Digital Citizenship: Introduce digital citizenship to stakeholders; focus on understanding what the strategic goal and initiatives are going to accomplish.

2010–11

Web 2.0 Integration: Increase the number of classrooms using Web 2.0 tools and the number of online resources available for teachers and students.

Mobile Learning: Expand mobile learning program to more campuses.

Digital Citizenship: Move stakeholders from understanding to acceptance of the strategic goal and initiatives.

2011–12

Web 2.0 Integration: Encourage districtwide Web 2.0 adoption; focus on teachers who have not yet used Web 2.0 tools.

Mobile Learning: Expand mobile learning program to more campuses.

Digital Citizenship: Instruct students on traditional digital citizenship elements, such as acceptable uses of technology and proper use of social networking sites.

BYOD: Use digital citizenship education to foster stakeholder understanding and acceptance of the district's BYOD program. Implement a districtwide BYOD program.

The pieces were beginning to fall into place; we now had a multiyear strategic plan that would address our objective of increasing student engagement. The next task was to define the critical success factors that would support each of these strategic initiatives.

CHAPTER 4

Success Factors
for Goal Achievement

At its core, the KISD strategic plan for mobile learning was less about the strategic initiatives themselves and more about changing our culture so the initiatives would become the new educational model for the district.

When talking about cultural changes such as these, a number of critical success factors must be in place for the changes to happen successfully. For KISD, we identified the following critical success factors to support our initiatives and, in turn, achieve our goal:

- Organizational commitment

- Organizational readiness

- Supportive people

- Technical infrastructure

- Support resources (This could not be on the back of administrators and teachers by themselves.)

- Administrative regulations (Changes in instructional delivery required regulation changes.)

- Measurement and review (We needed evaluation criteria to determine if the initiatives were accomplishing our goal of changing instruction.)

I want to discuss each of these critical success factors because they were crucial components in our mobile learning journey and were directly tied to the success we achieved. Additionally, these factors are often overlooked by educational systems interested in embarking on a mobile learning strategy.

Organizational Commitment

The type of cultural change we were planning would be disruptive, with plenty of bumps along the way. As a leadership team, our superintendent's cabinet needed to make sure we were committed to the plan and were willing to stand and defend the plan when issues arose. The commitment had to start with our superintendent. He needed to become visible and vocal about what we were doing and why we were doing it. He also had to be willing to defend it when necessary.

Our school board needed to support what we were doing and why. We all know that when teachers or parents get frustrated and don't like the district's answer, they call their school board member. We needed to make sure the school board was versed in the background of this strategic plan so that if and when the calls came in, they would be prepared to speak from a position of knowledge, not emotion.

As a cabinet, we knew that changing how our teachers taught would take commitment from multiple divisions within KISD. We did not want this three-year plan to be viewed merely as a "technology strategic plan"—it was a district strategic plan and would be presented as such, no matter the audience. We needed all cabinet members whose divisions had roles in the plan to become the champions and key communicators within their divisions. For our strategic plan, the key departments that were heavily involved from the beginning were technology, curriculum, and campus leadership.

One of the greatest risks when embarking on a plan such as this is inconsistent messaging. Those who are fighting the change will use inconsistent messaging as a reason to insert uncertainty, and once there is an undertone of uncertainty, it can become a serious impediment to progress. Because of this, we spent a lot of time on messaging, which was crucial in the early stages of rolling out our plan. We wanted to ensure that no matter who was talking, the message was the same, and our responses to questions or concerns were consistent.

Here is the message we shared with our stakeholders:

> A growing concern among our principals, teachers, students, and parents is student engagement. To address this concern, the district has set as its main goal to philosophically change the way instruction is delivered. We feel that by changing the way we instruct, we can improve student engagement.
>
> To achieve this goal, we have created a multiyear strategic plan consisting of three key initiatives. These initiatives are **Web 2.0 integration, mobile learning,** and **digital citizenship.** These initiatives together will enable us to implement a fourth initiative, a **BYOD program.**
>
> We understand changing instruction will not be easy and will take time. As a district, we are committed to supporting our campuses in this process.

Our commitment to the project started at the top with our superintendent, was reinforced by our school board, and was delivered throughout the district by cabinet members whose divisions had a role. Our message was consistent, with the foundation being a district plan, not a technology plan.

Organizational Readiness

Our initial communication regarding the strategic plan was focused on introducing the "why." We wanted there to be an understanding of what we were doing and what we were hoping to accomplish. We didn't focus on *how* we were going to accomplish the plan until there was an understanding of *what* the plan was going to accomplish. I think this is an important point and was one of the success factors in our early implementations of the three initiatives. Too often when introducing a cultural change, leaders of organizations try to communicate too much too fast. They assume the staff will understand and accept why the cultural change must occur, so they immediately start focusing on the tactical elements of the plan.

Without a clear understanding of the "why," human nature will not let our minds just accept change and move on. There has to be an emphasis on understanding first. People must be allowed to ask questions and voice concerns before they can move to the next "how" phase of a cultural change. The process of questioning and listening to concerns can be very difficult for some people. This part of the process often leads to defensiveness and impatience among project team members and can cause irreparable damage if rushed.

For these introductory meetings, a spokesperson must calmly listen and answer questions in such a way that audience members feel they have had an opportunity to participate and learn and walk away feeling their voices were heard. However, once any concerns are heard and, if necessary, addressed, everyone needs to understand the district is committed to this strategic goal and is moving ahead with it. It is a delicate balance for the spokesperson. He or she must show compassion to the difficulties of culture change, while showing commitment to the plan.

Supportive People

For KISD, the introduction of our plan started with our principals. Principals were the next level of leadership in our district beyond the superintendent's cabinet, a group of people who had very close ties to teachers, students, and parents. If we could foster understanding in our principals, they could assist in our messaging as we branched out to other stakeholder groups. We also understood that each campus has its own unique culture, and as we expanded our messaging, we would be less successful with a standard, pat message. By linking in the principals, we could leverage each unique campus culture and individualize our message to that culture.

Likewise, as we began talking with community members, we leveraged the relationship each principal had with his or her community to customize our message. Although there were custom messages for each campus, the content delivered was the same. Through this process of introducing our plan to the principals, teachers, and parents, we were able to gauge their organizational readiness. More important, we were able to identify the degree of cultural readiness for each campus, which was critical as we started thinking about the tactical rollout of our strategic plan. As you will see when we start discussing the individual initiatives in Part Two, the organizational readiness component dictated the pacing of implementation, which helped us better plan for and manage each year's expectations regarding the three-year plan.

Technical Infrastructure

Two of the three initiatives supporting our strategic goal (mobile learning and Web 2.0 integration) were directly affected by the technical infrastructure and its readiness to support the changes to instruction. As a result, we needed to make sure the infrastructure was capable of supporting these changes, was scalable to handle increased breadth and depth of use, and was reliable and capable of delivering the new resources to the classroom.

I often talked with our tech team about reliability. I wanted our technology infrastructure to be like light switches. When teachers turn on classroom light switches, they don't worry whether the lights are going to come on. I wanted our technology infrastructure to operate just as reliably. We had achieved that success with our existing infrastructure, and I wanted to ensure that as we changed the instructional tools teachers had at their disposal, the infrastructure's reliability wouldn't degrade.

Beyond the technical infrastructure capabilities, we needed new support tools that teachers could rely on as they worked to change how they were delivering instruction. We had to make the new

resources easily accessible anytime, anywhere for teachers. We needed
to establish online repositories that teachers could use for reference
materials.

We were planning professional development for teachers but knew
those training sessions would be limited. The last thing we wanted
was to pull teachers out of the classroom as part of the implementation. If face-to-face training was the only means teachers had at their
disposal to learn this new model of instruction, adoption of this new
philosophy would take a lot longer than three years.

Prepare Your Technology Department

As the person responsible for the district's Technology Department,
I knew our staff needed to understand what the next three years
would mean to our existing support model and mentality. However,
as I reflect on those three years, one of the things I did not do a good
job of was preparing my department for this new way of educating
teachers and students and fully appreciating its impact on our
existing support model and mentality. The old support models were
not flexible enough or quick enough to respond, especially in the early
stages when we were looking for early wins and success stories.

The old support model was one of control, standardization, and
evaluation, and was risk aversive. As we quickly learned, once implementation of the initiatives began, the Technology Department would
either help or hinder the success of these initiatives. We were changing
our support model on the fly to help these initiatives, but we did not
have a total understanding nor acceptance of the new instructional
model as it was being redefined and the impact it would have on the
various support models we were currently using.

Control, standardization, and evaluation were not abandoned; they
just took on a different look and feel in the new instructional model.
Where we got into trouble as a department was the risk aversion part
of the equation. As the new model was being redefined, those groups
responsible for control and standardization felt uncomfortable with
our new processes and were concerned that the changes were putting

our infrastructure at risk. The speed and frequency of change in the early phases of implementation was something my department was not familiar with or ready to accept.

Two groups were formed within the Technology Department. One group was tasked with pushing the envelope of innovation. They were responsible for identifying the new tools and defining how they would be used and how they would be introduced. The world of Web 2.0 is a very dynamic environment, and as you will learn in the Web 2.0 chapter (Chapter 5), this can be both a blessing and a curse.

The other group was responsible for control, standardization, and the overall technical reliability of our infrastructure. They were typically heavily involved in any new product evaluation and selection. Because this new suite of tools did not require any desktop installations, this group was often left out of the process until an issue was discovered or a change to our existing filtering parameters was being requested. Hence, this group felt like the controlled, secured environment we had worked so hard to establish over the previous five years was being compromised.

Both areas were doing exactly what I expected from them, but they didn't understand how they could coexist and still get the work done quickly without compromising the infrastructure. This caused a lot of disruption and unnecessary angst within our department. It could have been avoided had I spent time working with both divisions before implementation to define and establish the working parameters. We defined these parameters later in the process, only after the disruption had come to a head.

Support Resources

As luck would have it, the district was in the early stages of implementing a new financial and human resources package. Anytime you implement a new financial or human resources system, a critical success factor is the change-management process to help users of the system understand and accept the new processes and procedures.

For instance, one of the biggest change-management components is providing a support structure, which gives affected individuals an avenue to receive additional help and understanding as they struggle to adapt to the new system. The new package was districtwide, so we were able to leverage the change-management components into our own strategic instructional plan, and apply the same approach.

We knew this change of instruction was going to take a group effort far beyond the principal and teachers. We needed champions, cheerleaders, shoulders to cry on, and resources dedicated to the success of our initiatives. Principals and teachers are very resourceful and very skilled in the education of students, and given enough time they could adapt to this change of instruction. However, we were working with a three-year implementation timeline, and if we were going to start affecting student engagement, we needed the adoption process to begin immediately. We saw the need for a new team focused on pushing the initiatives and supporting our campuses.

A New Division from the Old

As a result, the superintendent's cabinet decided to create a new section within the Technology Department specifically focused on achieving our strategic goal and implementing the initiatives districtwide. Now, before you shake your head and say, "We can't add staff, so we can't do this" or "Well, KISD must be one of the wealthy school systems," let me explain where the resources for this new group came from.

Just like most school systems around the country, the budget for KISD was extremely tight and dwindling with each passing year. If we were going to create a new division, the resources within that division had to come from current KISD employees, and we would repurpose them into this new role. We looked at personnel across the district to find a subset who had classroom experience so they could relate to teachers, as well as a technology background and a passion for innovation. This was not an easy skill set to find without taking teachers from the classroom. As we searched for this group of people, we were also searching for their leader.

We needed a leader who could quickly get this new group off the ground, embrace the strategic goal, become an expert in the new resources, and be a champion for the implementation phase. This leader needed to have great communication skills because he or she would be front and center when introducing the initiatives to the various audiences. This leader would need to have a great working relationship with all the other departments outside the Technology Department. Though the Technology Department had a role in the implementation, this was not a technology strategic goal. It was a district goal with many departments having roles.

I was fortunate to have someone in my department who possessed the skill set we were looking for. The individual selected was a project manager for our campus technology retrofit program, and in her role had the opportunity to work closely with our principals and teachers. She had a passion for the classroom and experience teaching. Her working knowledge of our technology processes and procedures would be a huge asset, especially in the hectic early implementation phases. She was an individual who could quickly and easily establish a rapport with any type of audience, which was so important for this strategic goal—changing how teachers teach.

Rethinking Traditional Tech Support

Each of our campuses had an Instructional Technology Facilitator (ITF) as part of its campus staffing plan. For the secondary campuses, we had one ITF per campus. At the elementary level, we had one ITF for two campuses. Each ITF was supposed to help facilitate the integration of technology into classroom instruction. In reality, the ITF employees mostly served as campus technical support. The technical support role took so much time, little technology integration occurred systemically districtwide. However, our ITFs were ex-teachers who had a passion for technology and were the ones making requests to my department for any new technical ideas campuses or teachers might have. They were the perfect group of people to bring into the new division; they had both an interest in technology and experience in the classroom. With our new strategic plan, our ITFs would have opportunities to fulfill the functions ITFs were originally supposed to accomplish.

All we needed to do was introduce our ITFs to the strategic goal, make sure they understood and accepted it, have a clear implementation path forward, and let the innovation fly. The problem was the ITFs were already serving an important role on the campuses. The campuses would not be in favor of losing these services and resources. However, if you recall the first success factor listed in this section, Organizational Commitment, the cabinet felt this was an opportunity to once again emphasize our commitment from the top to this strategic goal. Even though this would have negative effects on the campus technology support environment, we believed the positive value in creating this division would outweigh the negative.

In our communication to the campuses, we emphasized the strategic plan and the impact these individuals would have on its success. We also talked about this being an opportunity for individuals on the campuses to become more self-sufficient from a technology perspective. Increased staffing was something we struggled with every year, and if our workforce could become more self-sufficient technologically, that would benefit everyone. Although it was a hard pill to swallow at first and was a message that needed constant reinforcement our first year, eventually campuses came to accept it. This was an issue we knew would be discussed more than once—in fact, it was discussed often by the principals and teacher groups. To his credit, our superintendent stood fast and never wavered on why the move was made and its value to the district in the long run.

We also were very empathetic that first year when listening to problems this move caused on campuses. While we stayed true to the reasoning, we also needed to show that we understood it was causing disruption. My department made some internal realignments to absorb the absence of these individuals and to help ease the disruption. We increased our training opportunities in some areas the ITFs had spent a lot of time supporting. We also monitored and tracked new work tickets coming into the system. We knew the majority of those tickets were a direct result of removing the ITFs, and it helped us plan opportunities for increased support or additional training opportunities. The ITFs moving into the new division were also concerned about the gap this move would cause on the campuses, and we discussed with them how we could help ease the transition.

That first year when these individuals were on campuses in their new role and questions came up related to their old role as an ITF, we wanted them to lend a helping hand. This greatly helped in the transition, because we knew it would be difficult for these individuals who once were the go-to people to all of the sudden now say, "I don't do that anymore. Let me call someone who can help you."

We now had our implementation group. Its primary responsibility was the implementation of our strategic goal. We felt these individuals were capable of taking on the challenges of cultural change, determined to succeed, and excited about the opportunities that lay ahead.

We called our new team "Instructional Technology," and they became part of the district's Technology Department. The 26 employees in this team were now instructional technology coordinators. You will learn in Part Two what role this group played for each initiative.

Administrative Regulations

When we started defining each of the initiatives, we quickly realized existing district regulations would need modification. Documents such as our acceptable use guidelines, student/employee code of conduct, and discipline management plans were all affected by the new initiatives. We also discovered a number of our forms needed more parental consent and explanation as we migrated into the Web 2.0 world. Changes to some of the regulations would require school board approval—we needed to identify those quickly and begin working on the modifications.

The problems were just like those our other stakeholders faced: the school board members needed time to understand and accept what this philosophical change meant to them as the governing body of the district. It was one thing to present our objective, strategic goal, and the initiatives involved; it was another for the board members to understand the administrative implications that would result from implementation. Just like our other stakeholders, acceptance and understanding evolved within our school board members, and pacing of the evolution was critical.

The way KISD chose to address policy changes allowed for flexibility, proof of concept, and expectation management. Rather than make wholesale changes to these regulations based on assumption and speculation, we used verbiage in the existing policies to "pilot" early stages of our plan, with policy modifications resulting from the pilot process. This process enabled KISD to make fact-based decisions based on real data and results.

As the phases of implementation progressed, so did regulation modifications, as well as understanding and acceptance from our school board, parents, and administrators. Because this new way of instructing students truly is an evolution, policy and regulation management really become "evergreen" processes that need special attention each year. All modifications were the results of our mobile learning, Web 2.0 integration, or BYOD initiatives and were integrated into our digital citizenship framework. In a later chapter on digital citizenship, you will read more about our modification process and the modifications we made to each of our documents.

Measurement and Review

One of the key elements when defining a strategic goal is to identify the measurement criteria that will be used to evaluate results, both positive and negative. When the strategic goal involves cultural change, identifying these measurement factors early, prior to any implementation, is even more important.

So, what kind of measurement criteria should an organization identify? KISD wanted criteria that would show results, validate these results, direct corrective action, justify continued courses of action, and allow for intervention when necessary. I don't believe these criteria are unique for measuring our specific strategic goal; in fact, we use these same criteria for all projects.

Show Results. We identified our strategic goal, to change how teachers teach, expecting the outcomes to be improved student engagement and achievement. We needed to identify measurement criteria that could show whether we were actually achieving the desired result. Each of our initiatives would have measurement data specifically tied to student achievement, but we wanted to measure the effects of changing instruction beyond student scores. As we worked through identifying criteria beyond grades, we came to the conclusion that we needed both tangible and intangible measurements for each of our initiatives. Tangible measurements include grades, attendance, and discipline. Intangible measurements include survey information from teachers, students, and parents related to engagement and enthusiasm.

Validate Results. Validation provides a means to measure and assess previous decisions. This validation helps foster support, not only for what the project has done but where it is heading. For KISD, changing instruction was affecting our stakeholders in very personal ways, and there would be a lot of questions, concerns, and opposition. Having measurement data to validate what we were doing and why we were doing it, as well as to illustrate the benefits resulting from this change, would help build a support base in all of our stakeholder groups. As we continued to build the support base, we also strengthened the willingness by all stakeholders to embrace this goal, embrace the change, and move ahead with the implementation objectives with a positive attitude.

Direct Corrective Actions. This type of measurement provides an opportunity to direct specific actions based on what the data shows. We all know that implementations ebb and flow, with many surprises along the way. Making smart use of measurement data allowed us to direct how specific activities occurred when these surprises happened.

Justify Continued Course of Action. Cultural change inherently brings with it that famous saying: "That's not how we do it." For cultural change to begin taking root, decisions must be made that change the way we did it before. Defining the right measurement criteria affords an organization the means to justify the decisions or course of action. This is critical when you are changing the way people have previously done their jobs. You are moving them out of their comfort zone and most assuredly will encounter pushback. Having the data to justify why you are taking a particular course of action helps reduce emotional negative responses and helps to build a more accepting attitude for future changes.

Allow Intervention When Necessary. When the measurement criteria are established, they afford the project team an opportunity to intervene when necessary. Intervening allows for proactive changes to the project, ensuring timelines and objectives continue to be met. It also provides the organization an opportunity to identify problem areas within the implementation and create specific action plans not only to address a particular issue, but keep the project on course, tactically and emotionally. Without measurement criteria, the project becomes reactive to issues arising from the implementation, which can be very costly not only from a timeline perspective, but from an emotional perspective.

So why do you measure? Simply put, when embarking on a strategic goal, particularly one involving cultural change, what gets measured gets managed.

Once the measurement criteria were identified, our next step was to define the specific data elements used in each category. For each of our strategic initiatives, we identified objectives that were milestones that would occur during the course of each phase of implementation. These milestones were significant accomplishments for each phase and would provide just-in-time measurements with data for each of the criteria.

We needed to define how each of the critical success factors, identified at the start of this chapter, was going to be measured. Critical success factors are often tracked by Key Performance Indicators (KPIs). A KPI tracks performance at a finely detailed level. In KISD we measured our KPIs using the following data sets. For each critical success factor, we identified a target result expectation. We then compared actual results against the target on a predetermined frequency. This comparison of expected results against actual results provided us with information specific to the measurement categories. In addition, it provided us with data from which we could forecast trends. Forecasting trends allowed us the opportunity to project implementation milestones and results well into the future. Having this information provided the implementation teams with a glimpse into the future and the opportunity to make course corrections.

For example, one milestone we tracked was teacher training and teacher readiness. After each of our training cycles, an evaluation was conducted with teachers, assessing their levels of understanding and readiness. Based on these assessments, we were able to adjust future training cycles to make them more effective.

Some of the measurement criteria we tracked from the training included understanding of our strategic goal and *why* the initiatives identified would help accomplish the goal. By tracking this measurement, we were able to identify the instructional technology team members who could best articulate the goal to teachers and those who were struggling to comprehend or share the message. We also tracked the training associated with our chosen Web 2.0 tools. One of the findings from that assessment was that teachers didn't just want training on how to use a Web 2.0 tool. They wanted specific training on how to use that Web 2.0 tool to teach their specific content areas, for example, using Animoto in seventh-grade English.

After we identified the categories of data we wanted to measure for each initiative, we needed to plan at a tactical level how we would gather the relevant data—through surveys, interviews, questionnaires, or by extracting data from the district computer systems. This process is often underestimated and not properly planned for. Unless you plan at a detailed level, assumptions are often made about the actual data gathering, and by the time you realize what those assumptions were and the resulting gaps in data gathering, you have lost precious time and, unfortunately, you have lost data.

For each initiative, we identified responsible individuals for each data area. We identified what computer systems the information would come from and in what type of format or report the information would be provided. The computer systems involved included the student information system, the learning management system, and the curriculum management system. We identified the individuals who would be responsible for data accuracy and data validation. The worst thing you can do is to provide inaccurate data for your measurement criteria. The minute your data become questionable, the measurement criteria identified above become invalid, and every move you make after that will be called into question. Your measurement of results and success will be continually questioned.

As you identify the specific data elements you need to measure, you must also discuss the frequency of the gathering process. More often may not be better when it comes to gathering data. Generating too much information may lead to those you intend to benefit becoming overwhelmed, frustrated, or just plain bored.

Additionally, you must identify the tools (such as software programs) required to report the information in a way that benefits their audiences. The level of detail will vary for each audience. We created measurement reports specific to each of our stakeholder groups— for instance, summary reports of milestones for the school board, training data sheets for teachers, and talking points and presentations for parent information nights. The tools we used varied depending on the information and type of data. We made extensive use of Microsoft Excel and PowerPoint.

Defining Your Measurement Criteria

Is that survey worth taking? Have you asked the same question too many times, in too many ways? Do you need that particular statistic? Use the following guidelines to determine whether each data point will provide you with useful, usable information.

Specific. Don't track data for data's sake. The information must be relevant to those reading the results and must serve a specific purpose.

Measurable. The information must be measurable and tied back to an expected result, action, or process. Measure even if the results are not good. If you show only positive results, the integrity of your measurement tracking process will come into question. Remember, the whole reason to measure is to provide a true representation. When results are not positive, it gives you the opportunity to explore why and make corrections to improve.

Attainable. Stretch targets and measures provide incentive for individuals being held accountable to work hard. We had stretch goals for the Instructional Technology Team, principals, and teachers. The key to setting stretch goals is to make them difficult but reachable. Unattainable targets and measurements will quickly demoralize those responsible and will not be a true reflection of what is occurring.

Time Dependent. For each measurement, there is a time frame during which the data should be tracked and reported. If the measurement is too frequent, there is little opportunity to show any change, either positive or negative. Likewise, if the duration is too long, there might be a drastic change but little information as to why the change occurred.

Overview of Each Strategic Initiative by School Year

Part Two of this book is divided into four chapters. Chapters 5, 6, and 7 describe how KISD implemented its Web 2.0 integration, mobile learning, and digital citizenship initiatives. These three initiatives built the foundation for KISD's three-year strategic plan. Chapter 8 describes how KISD leveraged the accomplishments of the foundational initiatives to implement the fourth initiative, bring your own device (BYOD).

In each chapter, the initiative is broken down into school year implementation phases. Within each yearly breakdown, I discuss the rollout of our plan, challenges and successes, the lessons we learned, and any surprises that necessitated a course correction leading into the next year.

On the following page is an outline of the yearly plans for our four strategic initiatives.

Web 2.0 Integration Initiative

2009–10: Introduce Web 2.0 to teachers at every campus.

2010–11: Increase the number of classrooms using Web 2.0 tools and the number of online resources available for teachers and students.

2011–12: Encourage districtwide Web 2.0 adoption; focus on teachers who have not yet used Web 2.0 tools.

Mobile Learning Initiative

2009–10: Pilot mobile learning with one grade at one campus.

2010–11: Expand mobile learning program to more campuses.

2011–12: Expand mobile learning program to more campuses.

Digital Citizenship Initiative

2009–10: Introduce digital citizenship to stakeholders; focus on understanding what the strategic goal and initiatives are going to accomplish.

2010–11: Move stakeholders from understanding to acceptance of the strategic goal and initiatives.

2011–12: Instruct students on traditional digital citizenship elements, such as acceptable uses of technology and proper use of social networking sites.

BYOD Initiative

2011–12: Use digital citizenship education to foster stakeholder understanding and acceptance of the district's BYOD program. Implement a districtwide BYOD program.

CHAPTER 5

Web 2.0 Integration Initiative

The superintendent's cabinet started working on the framework for our district's Web 2.0 integration initiative in the spring of 2009. As discussed in Chapter 4, the cabinet created a new section within the Technology Department, the Instructional Technology Team, whose focus was achieving our strategic goal and implementing the initiatives. The formalization of this group and achieving alignment to the strategic plan were our first priorities as we began planning for Web 2.0 integration.

2009–10 School Year

Getting the Instructional Technology Team on Board

Our first objective was to get the 26 members of our new Instructional Technology Team on board with the strategic goal. We spent a lot of time in the spring of 2009 talking with our new instructional technology coordinators about the goal and how we felt the strategic initiatives would help us to accomplish the goal. It was a useful process that gave us a glimpse into what some of the barriers would be with our stakeholders as we introduced each initiative.

Even though this new group comprised former teachers who had transitioned into technology support roles, their loyalty to the traditional education model was much more set in stone than expected. If our Web 2.0 implementation was going to succeed, this was the group that was going to make it happen. We needed to make sure we had 100 percent understanding and acceptance from these staff members, particularly in the early stages. Over the course of two months, we held many meetings with this group, discussing stakeholder feedback and their reactions to what was being said. I spent a lot of time talking about technology trends and how mobiles and cloud computing were changing the technology landscape. (See Chapter 1 for a discussion of these trends.)

It didn't take long for this group to come to the same conclusions the cabinet did. We talked about their role as technology integration coordinators and what their responsibilities would be. The group as a whole was very excited about the new role because they had become increasingly frustrated with their old role. Their old title was "technology facilitator," but as described in Chapter 4, there was very little integration occurring and a whole lot of technical support and equipment setup.

The most intriguing part of their new role was that of innovation. Giving this group of former teachers and technology advocates the opportunity to introduce innovation into the classroom was something they had wanted for a long time; the key was to control the innovation and ensure it was grounded in each of our initiatives.

Now that the Instructional Technology Team members were on board and excited about the goal, they began the next step: working at a tactical level to define the Web 2.0 implementation strategy for the start of the 2009 school year.

Defining the Web 2.0 Implementation Strategy

Our implementation strategy needed to be fairly simple if we wanted to have something in place for the start of the school year. The Instructional Technology Team and I needed to accomplish two things. First, we needed to create introductory sessions focusing on the basic concepts of Web 2.0 and how these tools could be incorporated into the classroom. Second, we needed to identify a set of Web 2.0 tools that we could take to each campus to introduce and model in a classroom setting for principals and teachers. With roughly three months to get this done, we needed to focus on basic concepts and tools most applicable to all grade levels—elementary, junior high, and high school. If we tried to focus on specific grade levels and curriculum areas, the introduction of Web 2.0 would not be districtwide and would drastically slow down our three-year implementation time frame. So we decided the Web 2.0 implementation objectives for the 2009–10 school year would be as follows.

The Instructional Technology Team would

- identify basic Web 2.0 concepts and how Web 2.0 tools can be used in the classroom.

- identify Web 2.0 tools applicable to any and all KISD classrooms.

- familiarize themselves with these tools so that they could introduce them to principals and teachers and model their uses.

- begin introducing these tools to the campuses beginning in September 2009.

In late May 2009, we started the process of defining basic Web 2.0 concepts and identifying potential Web 2.0 tools that we wanted to introduce into KISD classrooms. When we began defining introductory concepts, our focus was on things like the types of Web 2.0 tools, grade level appropriateness, classroom management, and what KISD was going to offer in the way of Web 2.0 options.

The Web 2.0 environment is massive with so many tools available—one of the most dynamic environments I have experienced in my career as a technology professional. It didn't take long for the identification process to spin out of control. It seemed like there was a "Web 2.0 tool of the day," and we were not making progress toward actually identifying the tools we were going to introduce to teachers for use in the upcoming school year.

We spent about two weeks in this helter-skelter mode and were not meeting milestones we'd established for creating KISD's Web 2.0 environment. So we used the missed milestones as an opportunity to stop and reevaluate our selection process.

In order to streamline the tool selection process, we needed to embrace the dynamic nature of the Web 2.0 environment and come to terms with the fact that there would always be a new tool or new functionality. We needed to make decisions *now* and stop trying to manage the ever-changing world of Web 2.0. I told the Instructional Technology Team to make decisions based on what they knew at that moment. If we looked back on our decisions in the future and saw they were wrong, that was OK. This is the world of technology—if you wait for things to stop changing, decisions will never be made.

During our reevaluation, we also realized that the Curriculum Department had to be part of our Web 2.0 tool selection process. (In our district, this department is officially titled the Teaching and Learning Department but is referred to as the Curriculum Department here.) KISD had worked very hard to establish a standardized curriculum districtwide. This standardized curriculum provided the same learning opportunities and tools for each student no matter what campus he or she attended. We needed to have support from the Curriculum Department for instructional tools being introduced into the classroom; otherwise, it could be perceived that Web 2.0 integration was a technology initiative, not a district initiative.

Another need emerged during this time. We needed a mechanism to create a pool of Web 2.0 tools that we expected teachers to use. To address this need, we created the KISD Web 2.0 toolbox. This toolbox would be the source from which teachers could select Web 2.0 tools to incorporate into their classrooms. Creating this toolbox would make the process of incorporating these new educational resources very easy. Teachers would not have to go out onto the web and search to find a recommended tool; they would simply access the toolbox on our school website.

The time we took to reevaluate our Web 2.0 approach saved us time in the long run. Once we resolved the issues, the process of identifying potential tools became much more efficient.

In our new process, when a potential tool was identified for our toolbox, it went through a vetting process. Three separate groups reviewed each tool. Two groups from the Technology Department were involved in the vetting process, the Instructional Technology Team and the Technology Operations Group. The Instructional Technology Team reviewed the tool from the perspective of what we had, functionality duplication, age appropriateness, and ease of use. The Technology Operations Group evaluated the tool from an infrastructure standpoint to ensure compliance with our technical standards. The final group in the vetting process was the Curriculum Department. They reviewed each tool to ensure alignment with our instructional standards and alignment with our existing curriculum resources and content delivery processes.

Our preference when we started to identify potential tools was to select ones that were free; however, as we began evaluating the free tools, a new challenge with Web 2.0 quickly emerged—access control.

Access Control Issues

The suite of education tools students were currently using in the classroom could only be accessed by KISD students through a network authentication process and were unavailable to anyone outside the KISD system. However, when we began exploring the Web 2.0 world, we found that access control varied depending on the tool. We identified two types of Web 2.0 tools with three levels of access control:

- Free tools with no access control
- Free tools with limited access control based on individual teacher configuration
- Subscription-based tools with district-level access control

We also found that some of the Web 2.0 tools had two communities for end users. One community was identified as "public use," which meant anyone on the Internet could access and use it. The other community was an "education" classification that was geared toward educational end users. So, our selection process, once thought to be fairly simple, had levels of complexity we did not expect.

Our challenge when trying to address access control was twofold. First, we had a limited budget available for the Web 2.0 portion of the project; therefore, selecting only tools with a subscription-based application was not an option. Second, we did not know what the adoption rate in the district would be for these tools, and I was apprehensive about paying for district subscriptions and then not having those tools fully used. At this point, we reevaluated our initial strategy of selecting tools applicable to all grade levels.

Because of the variations in access control with these tools, we changed our selection criteria from applicability to all grade levels to applicability to elementary and applicability to secondary. This change resulted in the creation of two separate toolboxes: one for our elementary teachers and one for our secondary teachers. The elementary toolbox would consist mostly of Web 2.0 tools that had subscription-based, district-level access control along with some teacher-level access control. Our secondary toolbox would have tools based on subscription or teacher-level access control, but for our older students we would also introduce some tools with no access control. For example, with a tool like Glogster, at the elementary level teachers would create accounts for their classrooms; however, at the high school level, students would create their own accounts.

We divided the Instructional Technology Team into two teams. One team would focus on tools for elementary grades and the other team would focus on tools for secondary grades. Our priority would be to first look at tools that applied to both age groups and then move to the specific elementary or secondary tools. With our new selection strategy in place, we began the identification process once again.

When a Web 2.0 tool had been vetted and put into one of the toolboxes, we stopped looking at any other tools that provided the same base functionality.

Managing the Toolboxes

Once we started putting Web 2.0 tools into the toolboxes, we needed to begin working on sample lessons and modeling strategies for each tool. We subdivided the two teams—within each team (elementary and secondary), one group was responsible for the continued identification and vetting of potential tools, and one group was responsible for creating sample lessons and modeling strategies.

Having the Instructional Technology Team staffed with former teachers, either from the elementary or secondary level, helped when we started developing sample lessons to introduce Web 2.0 tools to the campuses. During the lesson creation process, we identified a potential barrier to achieving widespread Web 2.0 adoption. If Web 2.0 adoption was going to depend on the 26 people from Instructional Technology and their ability personally to reach 32 campuses and 2,500 teachers, this would be a long road. We needed a resource beyond face-to-face meetings where teachers could view sample lessons or find "how-to" information. We needed a knowledgebase.

Developing a Knowledgebase

Knowledgebase is a computer technology term for an information repository that provides a means for information to be collected, organized, shared, searched, and used. We wanted our Web 2.0 knowledgebase to house lessons and modeling strategies, as well as provide simple "how-to's" for each of the Web 2.0 tools in the toolboxes.

We began immediately to develop this knowledgebase so that teachers could have access at the start of the school year. We knew this resource would help speed adoption of Web 2.0 tools within our district.

Additionally, as teachers began integrating these tools and developing their own lessons, we could take their lessons and include them within the knowledgebase. With this resource, our support base could grow as each new teacher adopted Web 2.0 tools.

Over the next two and a half months, we created the elementary and secondary toolboxes and developed lessons and modeling strategies for each. By early August, we had enough information gathered to put our knowledgebase into production.

Introducing the Tools to Principals and Teachers

During that same two-and-a-half-month period, the Instructional Technology director and I began having conversations with our principals, introducing them to our district strategy and talking about Web 2.0 tools and the implementation plan for the start of school. We needed to have support and understanding from our principals for the strategy and initiatives that we were going to kick off at the start of school. As I mentioned before, leadership was going to be one of the keys to making this strategy of changing instruction successful.

For the most part, our principals were receptive to the goal of changing instruction. But their uneasiness started to emerge when we talked about the initiatives themselves. Using Web 2.0 tools in the classroom was a relatively new concept, so getting total buy-in from this group was not going to happen with just a few conversations. My goal during this time was simply to introduce our plan and get their support for introducing the toolboxes at each of their campuses. Without a doubt, our principals supported introducing the toolboxes. The question was what role they would take in encouraging the adoption of Web 2.0 throughout their campuses.

In mid-August, as the school year approached, my biggest concern, based on conversations with principals, was how we could get teachers excited about and willing to try the Web 2.0 tools. The last couple of weeks before the start of school, we spent a lot of time talking about the introduction sessions. How would we introduce the tools? How would we demonstrate the value of the tools? How would we make this new way of teaching exciting and not scary? We knew we had one shot with teachers, and we didn't want to miss the opportunity or send the wrong message. We knew that each level—elementary, junior high, and high school—had its own culture, and in some cases each campus had its own culture. If we created a single approach for the introduction, those cultural differences could be a barrier to adoption.

So, we created an introduction template but customized the presentation for each level and, if necessary, each campus based on its particular culture. Having staff in the Instructional Technology Team who had come directly from the campuses helped with customization.

Once the presentations were finalized for elementary, junior high, and high school, we spent a lot of time practicing and doing mock sessions. The mock sessions were in front of various audiences, including some principals. These provided the group opportunities to practice their messaging, fine tune any points of confusion, and get comfortable with the content and their roles as ambassadors for the initiative.

The Introduction Process

Beginning in October, we started the introduction process at our campuses. The Instructional Technology Team scheduled time at every campus to introduce Web 2.0 concepts and tools. Prior to the campus meetings, the team met with each principal to review the presentation and discuss the intended outcomes. This proved to be valuable, as the principals set the tone for the meeting as well as defined what their expectations were.

The Instructional Technology Team spent the first part of the presentation introducing the basic concepts of Web 2.0 and explaining that Web 2.0 integration was a key initiative in the district's three-year strategic plan. The second half of the presentation was focused on the Web 2.0 toolboxes; we briefly reviewed the tools in them and how they could be used in various instructional settings. The tone of the meeting was critical; we did not want the teachers to feel threatened by the tools and went to great lengths to explain these were simply tools we wanted them to try. They were not being forced to use any of the tools right away, and, most important, they had a support team (Instructional Technology) there to help them when they did decide to use the tools in their classrooms. To my great surprise and pleasure, generating excitement for the tools and finding teachers willing to try the tools was not an issue at any of our 32 campuses. I believe this is a credit to our Instructional Technology Team and the way they went about introducing both the strategy of changing instruction and the Web 2.0 toolboxes.

At every campus, we found teachers who were immediately willing to incorporate the Web 2.0 tools into their classrooms. Actually, some of these teachers already had been incorporating Web 2.0 tools, but because the district had not embraced or endorsed Web 2.0, they felt like they would be viewed negatively, so it was not something they discussed openly.

I think it is important to understand that the Web 2.0 introduction process was the beginning of our cultural change process in KISD. We were now talking about ways teachers were going to instruct in their classrooms differently. At its core, instructional delivery is the culture of an educational system. When you attempt to change instructional delivery, you are changing a culture. Changing an organization's culture is challenging in and of itself, but changing this type of culture becomes personal for your key stakeholders—teachers. You must be realistic about the adoption cycles for this change. You will never have 100% adoption in Year One, and forcing this type of change on your teachers is a recipe for failure. When you embark on changing the instructional delivery model, you will have three distinct camps of teachers:

Early Adopters. These are teachers who embrace the change enthusiastically.

Testers. These are teachers who are willing to try some new things but will use the old instructional model as much as the new model.

Resisters. These are teachers who, for whatever reasons, have not embraced the new model and are going to fight the change.

The smallest camp, by far, is the early adopters, yet they are the most influential. If you try to force the testers and resisters into immediate adoption, they will push back, and resistance from this larger group could derail your program. The smarter approach is to focus on the early adopters in Year One and begin to leverage their ability to influence the other two camps in subsequent years. If you take this realistic approach and use the people with the most influence to your advantage, the tester and resister numbers will decrease with each passing year. Ultimately, three to four years down the road, the resisters (however many there are left) may need to go if they cannot embrace the change or the district's goals.

Focus on Early Adopters

Because KISD had early adopters at every campus, and this group was big enough to keep the Instructional Technology Team busy with their support, we decided to focus solely on these individuals that first year. Another aspect of focusing on these early adopters was our desire to build a support base the first year. By having enthusiastic early adopters at every campus, we were increasing our ambassador pool, which was one of our first-year objectives.

With these early adopters, adoption of the Web 2.0 tools and their integration into classroom instruction occurred very quickly. This was incredibly beneficial because the majority of the first year spent in the Web 2.0 environment was focused on creating lessons and working through some of the tool issues with this group of highly motivated and excited teachers.

The information in our knowledgebase grew exponentially that first year. The work being put into that resource came not only from the Instructional Technology Team, but the early adopters as well. Because of the outstanding work the early adopters were producing, we wanted to recognize this very special group of teachers. Competition is one of the greatest motivators when it comes to getting people's attention, so we established the districtwide Digital Star Teacher award. Digital Star Teachers were awarded and recognized throughout the course of a school year at each of our levels—elementary, junior high, and high school. We used this opportunity to showcase the Web 2.0 tools and resulting changes in instruction that were occurring in the winners' classrooms. We also used it as an opportunity to recognize leadership at the campuses, understanding that without their support we would not have seen these results.

At the end of the first year using Web 2.0, we announced Digital Star Teachers of the Year. With each recognition, we were getting teachers' attention, and the teachers started asking how they could get their names thrown into the hat to be considered the next go-round. It was just another way for us to inspire excitement for the toolboxes and show the amazing things that could occur in classrooms taking advantage of this new instructional resource.

Throughout our first year, we established and charted milestone checkpoints to ensure the Web 2.0 initiative was accomplishing our goal of changing instruction. At each of the milestone checkpoints, the feedback received from our group of early adopters absolutely supported our premise that introducing Web 2.0 tools into the classroom would help achieve our goal of changing instruction and improving student engagement. The teachers using these tools talked about student engagement immediately improving within their classrooms. The work being produced by the students using these tools was at a higher level than it had been when they used traditional paper and pencil.

I visited with some of these teachers, and they talked about how the work they were receiving from students using the Web 2.0 tools was typically what they saw for extra credit or from just a small portion of their students. They talked about how these tools tapped into creativity they never would have seen from some students had they just been using traditional tools.

The teachers were amazed by how much integrating these tools into their classrooms facilitated student collaboration. These tools naturally enabled collaboration without teachers having to plan for how it would occur. It is important to note that although we introduced our Web 2.0 toolboxes to all teachers, we never mandated their use or pushed these tools as a total replacement for paper-and-pencil instruction. What we did talk about in the introduction and throughout the first year was that there is a time and place in instruction for Web 2.0 tools, and there is a time and place for traditional tools. Our early adopters were successful in finding the appropriate time for each type of instruction.

Surprisingly, that first year we didn't have any significant issues related to access control. We identified some minor tweaks and enhancements that first year, and we worked with a number of our Web 2.0 vendors to fine-tune some of their administration tools. Vendors of the tools that we had incorporated into our toolboxes were more than willing to work with us to make their products better, knowing that issues we faced more than likely would be issues other school systems would encounter when trying to use their products.

At the end of the first year implementing Web 2.0, we evaluated the results. Our expectation was Web 2.0 tools would facilitate a change of instruction. We wanted to introduce the toolbox at every campus and get a small subset of teachers at each level—elementary, junior high, and high school—using the tools in their classrooms. To determine if there had been a beneficial change in instruction, we used observational data from our Instructional Technology Team as well as feedback from the early adopters about the effect, Web 2.0 tools had on their instructional delivery. This data clearly indicated that Web 2.0 tools in the classroom were changing how instruction was delivered. By looking at participation rates, we found that not only did we have adoption by a subset of teachers at each level, we also had adoption by a subset of teachers at every campus. Given that we had early adopters at each campus successfully utilizing Web 2.0 tools in their classrooms, it was determined Year One was a success, and it was time to focus on Year Two.

2010–11 School Year

Our primary objective for the second year was to increase the number of classrooms using Web 2.0 tools (the breadth of Web 2.0 tool use) and the number of online resources available for teachers and students (the depth of Web 2.0 tool use).

Evaluating the Toolboxes

As we began planning our summer work for the start of our second year using Web 2.0 tools, our focus was on evaluating the existing tools in the toolboxes and making necessary additions, changes, or deletions to our current offerings. If we wanted to provide the tools that best met the needs of our users, we couldn't afford to let our toolset become static in the dynamic Web 2.0 world. One thing we did throughout the first year was to emphasize to our teachers, especially the early adopters, that the Web 2.0 world was constantly changing and remind them not to get hooked on a single tool that might be gone next year. We wanted everyone to understand that continual changes to the toolboxes were going to be a necessity.

We also took the opportunity to evaluate the subscription-based tools. We increased the number of district seats available based on usage numbers from the previous year and projections for growth for this school year. The nice part about the subscription-based tools was that we could use the previous year's data to increase budgets where necessary, in anticipation of an expanded user base.

We received input from our group of early adopters regarding each tool. The feedback told us what the users liked about the tools, what they didn't like, and what Web 2.0 functionality was missing or one they would like to take advantage of as they started their second year. This feedback was invaluable as we began the process of evaluating our toolboxes. With the teacher feedback in hand, we looked for tools that would address their concerns and requests.

The input received from elementary teachers indicated the tools in our elementary toolbox were meeting their needs and required very few changes. The main issue our elementary teachers struggled with was the number of individual accounts required for each of our tools. Having to manage so many individual accounts made it cumbersome to use multiple tools in a classroom setting. Finding tools that would provide consolidated functionality under one application would greatly streamline their instruction.

Feedback on the secondary toolbox was different. High school teachers felt many of the tools were too simple or more appropriate for younger students. They wanted us to find tools that allowed for more freedom and access to more information relevant to high school students and the adult topics they were researching or studying. So our secondary toolbox looked quite different as we prepared for the start of the next school year.

Leveraging the Early Adopters

Beyond the toolbox changes, we spent the summer formulating strategies to leverage the skills and enthusiasm of our group of early adopters to increase the breadth and depth of Web 2.0 use by other teachers. We wanted this group of teachers to become champions for the Web 2.0 initiative and take over the push to use these tools on their campuses. More important, we wanted to expand the influence of these early adopters beyond their individual campuses.

As teachers are much more receptive and comfortable learning and asking questions among peers rather than with someone from the central office, our idea was to bring early adopters together with their peers to showcase and discuss how Web 2.0 tools could be used in a classroom. The problem was, we could not pull these teachers from their classrooms to conduct training sessions, and even if we could, when would the training occur? Not wanting to dismiss this opportunity, we began looking at virtual options available for the district that would allow teachers to remain on their campuses and still receive training and mentoring or ask questions.

We chose Adobe Connect as our virtual meeting resource and started planning sessions for various grade and subject levels. If we could get a fifth grade science early adopter to host an Adobe Connect session with other fifth grade science teachers to discuss using Web 2.0 in an upcoming lesson, breadth and depth of use surely had to increase. The standardized curriculum established in our district would make virtual meetings easier. Each campus was teaching with the same scope and sequence, so providing just-in-time training meant that teachers could attend the Adobe Connect sessions and see how Web 2.0 tools were going to be used for their own upcoming lessons. They could immediately walk away with something to work on.

We also created "Webinar Wednesdays," hosted by individuals from the Instructional Technology Team, for anyone to attend. At Webinar Wednesdays, teachers could see examples and applications of Web 2.0 tools in action. The sessions were recorded and stored in our knowledgebase and could be easily accessed by anyone not able to attend an online session.

With our toolbox changes complete and our strategies in place for increasing breadth and depth of Web 2.0 tool use, we were ready for the start of the second year.

In October of the new school year, we began meeting with the early adopters to discuss our strategies on how we could leverage their knowledge and skills. It was amazing to see how excited these groups of teachers were about their new role. Teachers as a whole are very collaborative and want to share, so asking this group to become champions for our Web 2.0 integration initiative wasn't a hard sell. They were more than willing to take the leadership role on their campuses and were equally enthused when we talked about how

Adobe Connect sessions would give them an opportunity to share with teachers districtwide.

By the end of October, we were already holding districtwide Adobe Connect sessions, hosted by our early adopter teachers. We began meeting with teachers at individual campuses and showcasing early adopters from their campuses who were leveraging Web 2.0 tools. We started conducting the Webinar Wednesdays in November. We thought the year was going just as planned. Then reality hit; nothing could be this easy!

Curriculum Concerns

As the school year moved along, we began to hear rumblings from the Curriculum Department regarding the quality of instruction that was occurring using the Web 2.0 tools. Now, we had done a good job in our first year of including the Curriculum Department in the vetting process for the Web 2.0 tools. What we did not do a good job of was working with that same department as we created the lessons and modeling strategies. While we did a great job of working with the teachers on the use of Web 2.0 tools, we did nothing when it came to the curriculum specialists.

The rumblings quickly moved from just noise to something that could turn into a barrier to the success of this initiative. If a rift developed between the Instructional Technology Team and the Curriculum Department, that division would spread like wildfire throughout the district and grind this initiative to a halt. We decided to address the concerns, establish a corrective plan of action, and make sure both departments were comfortable with the plan. Despite the problems, the working relationship between the two departments remained good, and this established relationship allowed us to work successfully through the issues. At no time during this process was there finger pointing or a hint of wanting to abandon the Web 2.0 toolset.

The first concern we had to address was the perception that instruction being delivered using Web 2.0 tools did not meet the standards

KISD had established. Were the tools enabling the proper core understandings, or were the tools simply new "toys" that students liked to use? To get to the root of this question, the curriculum specialists needed to understand the tools and how they were being applied in the classrooms. If they didn't understand the functionality of the tools and what teachers were doing with them, they could not make a judgment call on their effectiveness. So, the first thing we did was dedicate instructional technology resources experts to work side by side with curriculum specialists. We needed both departments to understand each other's perspective and learn from each other. Additionally, this would help the curriculum specialists understand the Web 2.0 tools so that as they were writing curriculum, they could incorporate the tools.

My department did not immediately accept this approach. Some were concerned that dedicating our resources to this effort would slow down the strategic plan implementation timeline by limiting Web 2.0 adoption. This was a valid concern; however, I knew if we let this misalignment continue between the two departments, the ramifications would be far worse than simply slowing down. I also reminded the group about the early adopters. It was a fact that the breadth-and-depth goal for Year Two might not reach the target levels we originally hoped for, but progress toward the initiative would not completely stop. The early adopters were still out there carrying the water and taking a leadership role toward the Year Two objective.

The second area we focused on was the actual instruction being delivered in classrooms. It is important to understand that instructional delivery was a concern for our district far beyond those teachers using Web 2.0 tools. Quite honestly, it is a concern for every education system in the country. So we worked closely with the Curriculum Department as it identified processes to address instructional delivery. As curriculum experts defined these processes, we carried the ball as it related to Web 2.0 instruction. Our task was to ensure their goal of improving overall instruction was being accomplished through the use of the Web 2.0 toolbox.

The time we took to address this alignment issue probably slowed down progress toward the Year Two goal. However, alignment issues between the Instructional Technology Team and the Curriculum Department didn't resurface.

Parental Concerns

Oh, but we aren't done with bumps in the road that occurred during Year Two! As we reviewed our first year using Web 2.0 tools, one surprise was how little we heard from parents in the form of resistance or concerns. I think in the first year, because Web 2.0 was so new and not widely used beyond the early adopters, it flew under the parental radar screen. As the breadth and depth of use increased in Year Two, parental concerns began to surface.

Parental concerns in Year Two can be categorized into three areas:

1.   access control

2.   inappropriate content

3.   age restrictions

Access control. Access control, particularly for Web 2.0 tools that required individual teacher configuration, was the first concern that surfaced in Year Two. For some tools, access control was determined by individual teachers. Some of the Web 2.0 tools required that each teacher create a classroom within that tool and assign their students to that classroom. We discovered through conversations with parents that, as a district, we were not consistent when it came to defining how students would be given access to a particular Web 2.0 tool's classroom. In some cases, generic IDs and passwords were created for all the students in the class. In other cases, individual IDs and passwords were assigned to each student. Parents were concerned about the generic access method. They were concerned about the privacy of their children's work as well as the possibility for work to be deleted or changed by other students. While we had not experienced any of these issues, their concerns were valid and needed to be addressed.

As a result of our discussions with parents, we determined that the district needed to define setup procedures for tools that required individual teacher access control configuration. The standard for our district would be to eliminate the generic ID and password configuration. Once the setup procedures were identified, we worked with our Web 2.0 vendors to identify the teachers using the affected tools. We then met with these teachers to make sure they had their virtual classrooms configured properly. It was a positive and productive process to meet with parents, listen to their concerns, and collectively come up with a resolution. It was very much a give-and-take process. Happily, both sides were able to meet in the middle and define an acceptable path forward.

Inappropriate content. The next parental concern was the ability for children to access inappropriate content via the Web 2.0 tools. As I mentioned earlier, some of the tools had two types of user communities. One community was open to everyone on the Internet, independent of age or type of use. Inappropriate content on the public community section of those tools was definitely a possibility. Students would purposefully have to seek out and search for inappropriate content—nonetheless, it could be accessed.

The other community was for educational use only. Users of that community were school children and teachers. The education community was much more restrictive; in most cases, the vendor would patrol the content and remove anything inappropriate. In addition to vendor monitoring, customers could call the vendor to review and consider deleting questionable content, as well. We all know the world of the Internet, and while the vendor and KISD were actively monitoring this community, the likelihood of inappropriate content within the education community was still a possibility. Also, some of the content within the education community was appropriate for some age groups and inappropriate for others.

As we started to research this parental concern, we discovered that some of our teachers were using the public community as the location for their classrooms rather than the educational community. In those situations, we immediately worked with those teachers to get their classrooms into the education community. Once again our Web 2.0 vendors were very helpful in identifying which community a teacher's classroom was in. We made changes to our communication packets for that particular tool to highlight the proper configuration, and we made changes to our knowledgebase. The real heart of this parental concern was inappropriate content in the education community and what we (KISD) were going to do to eliminate the possibility.

I discuss how we chose to answer the fundamental parental concern about access to inappropriate content in Chapter 7, "Digital Citizenship." Here I will just say that we as a school system did everything we could to provide an environment free from inappropriate content. But for those of us in the trenches, we know this is a losing battle. I don't know any technology leader who would stand up and say their environments are 100 percent free from inappropriate content or 100 percent impervious to viruses. We implement all the best practices, utilize proactive monitoring, and work with our hardware and software vendors diligently. The fact remains, if someone wants to find inappropriate content on the Internet, he or she can and will find that content. As an education system, we needed to provide the learning mechanisms such that digital citizenship is central to every classroom, and appropriate disciplinary actions result when someone chooses to misbehave.

This is a tough reality for some parents to accept and to me highlights the digital divide that continues to widen with some of the parents. Children need to be monitored while they are on the Internet, and if they are left on their own, bad things can happen.

In some cases, the district worked with parents and was able to foster an understanding and acceptance of our philosophy. In other cases, we could not reach that level of understanding and just had to agree to disagree.

Age restrictions. The final parental concern that arose in Year Two was access to some Web 2.0 tools and their associated age restrictions. The Children's Online Privacy Protection Act (COPPA) of 1998 stipulates that a "child" is anyone under of the age of 13 and anyone 13 years or older is defined as an "adult" when it comes to using Internet websites. What this means for parents is if their child is deemed an adult by COPPA standards, they do not have rights to access that child's account. Parents cannot call the Internet vendor and request passwords or tell them to delete their child's account. The child is considered an adult and is protected. As we would quickly find out, COPPA was something most parents were unfamiliar with, and it became a key component of our digital citizenship program as it related to parents. COPPA had an impact for KISD because of the age restrictions some of the Web 2.0 tools had established for users of their products.

Before rolling out Web 2.0 tools, the district had a few software packages that had an age restriction of 13 or older. We determined that this software was appropriate for our younger students. However, for KISD to allow our younger students access to these software packages, we needed to obtain parental consent. This parental consent was obtained via our student enrollment forms. Parents filled out these forms at the beginning of each year for each of their students. On the enrollment form, one checkbox gave approval for students to go on the Internet; another checkbox allowed students to use Internet sites deemed acceptable by KISD. A final checkbox obtained parental approval for younger students to access websites with the 13-year-old restriction. We had never had an issue relating to these sites and younger students accessing them until we rolled out Web 2.0 tools.

As the number of teachers using our toolboxes increased, we started getting calls from parents wanting information, such as:

- What tools would be used in their child's classroom?
- How were the tools being used?
- How could they learn more about the tools?
- How was access to the tools being controlled or managed?
- How would we use tools that had an age requirement of 13 or older at the elementary level?

On the plus side, we were starting to increase community awareness of the instructional changes occurring in our classrooms. The downside was that a lot of misinformation circulated related to the tools. We needed to quickly make information available to the parents, providing answers to their questions and redirecting the misinformation that was beginning to build.

We decided to create within our elementary and secondary student portals (accessible to parents) a Web 2.0 Tools section. Within this section, we would identify every tool available to the children. We provided a link to the tool's website with an overview of what the tool did and how it was being used in the classroom.

For each of our tools, we created an age-appropriate rating system similar to that used for movies. This rating system would indicate any age restrictions the site might have. It also indicated whether classroom configuration was at the district level, teacher level, or open (see Figures 5.1 and 5.2). This was one of the most beneficial information banks we created throughout the entire project. Once we put this on our website and directed parents to it, their questions and concerns dramatically reduced. I will not say all concerns completely went away. With some parents we had to agree to disagree, and we still heard from them. But on the whole, this information bank answered most of the questions parents had.

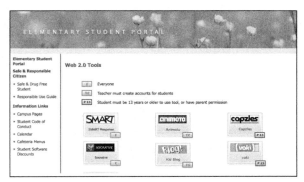

FIGURE 5.1   Sample of Web 2.0 Tools section of Katy ISD's Elementary Student Portal (www.katyisd.org/sites/sp/ele/Pages/Web20.aspx)

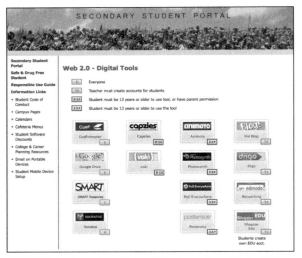

FIGURE 5.2   Sample of Web 2.0 Tools section of Katy ISD's Secondary Student Portal (www.katyisd.org/sites/sp/sec/Pages/DigitalTools.aspx)

While our student portals provided much of the information parents were requesting, there was still a lingering question about parental approval for younger students accessing tools with a 13 or older age restriction. To address this issue, we needed to go back to the enrollment form and clarify meanings of the age restriction and approval parents were actually granting by checking the box. We modified the enrollment form to include clarifying verbiage—this has greatly reduced the confusion related to age-restricted websites. The enrollment form now states:

Internet, Web Tools, and Email Access

Filtered Internet access is provided to KISD students as defined by the Children's Internet Protection Act (CIPA). Access will be supervised by District teachers or staff.

If your child is under 13 years of age, the Children's Online Privacy Protection Act (COPPA) requires additional parental permissions for some educational applications accessible over the Internet. All KISD students in grades 6–12 will receive a student email account. If you do not want your student to have access to the Internet, use educational applications accessible over the Internet, or have a KISD email address, please contact your student's campus principal with written notice. For more information regarding these tools, see the "Responsible Use Guidelines" section of the Discipline Management Plan and Student Code of Conduct.

We also made this a nonnegotiable topic when talking with parents in our digital citizenship programs.

Evaluation

As the school year wound down, we paused to evaluate Year Two of the Web 2.0 integration initiative. Our evaluation came from two perspectives: Did we achieve the expected results as they related to the district's strategic goal (changing how teachers teach)? Did we achieve the expected results for the Web 2.0 integration initiative that were established for the second year (increase the number of classrooms using Web 2.0 tools and the number of online resources available for teachers and students)?

At the district level, when we analyzed Year Two of the Web 2.0 integration initiative and its impact on changing instruction, we once again used observational data from the Instructional Technology Team as well as feedback from those teachers who were utilizing the tools. The data from teachers was particularly interesting because we had input from teachers in their second year of using the tools as well as teachers who were in their first year of adoption. The results of observation and teacher feedback mimicked those seen in the first year. Web 2.0 tool use was still changing instruction and improving student engagement. Students' experiences and the quality of their work were also similar to that seen in our first year (more engagement and better quality). The feedback provided by teachers using the tools validated this initiative and its role in changing instruction. We found that we were meeting our objective of increasing the number of classrooms using Web 2.0 tools through observations from the Instructional Technology Team and through the higher number of Web 2.0 tool-related support requests from campuses. We also had increased the number of online resources available to teachers significantly from the first year.

We had continued the Digital Star Teacher recognition program through Year Two. The award was something every campus was keenly aware of, and was a significant motivator for teachers using the selected Web 2.0 tools.

We also learned in Year Two that alignment between the Instructional Technology Team and Curriculum Department needed to be a priority. The alignment of these two departments ensured that the staff responsible for the district curriculum had a working knowledge of the Web 2.0 toolset and could incorporate the toolset into the curriculum as it was being developed. In addition, the alignment would ensure instructional-delivery concerns were being addressed for all classrooms, not just classrooms using Web 2.0 tools.

Although we made significant gains in the number of new teachers using our toolbox, we did not meet our target. The main reason we were unable to reach our target was the redirection of instructional technology resources from classroom teachers to individuals in the Curriculum Department. This shifted a lot of work to the shoulders of the early adopters and the Adobe Connect sessions. However, the benefits we achieved by redirecting resources to support the Curriculum Department far outweighed the downside of not reaching our target numbers.

In addition to the measures highlighted above, the second year was considered successful when it came to parent-school interactions and addressing parents' concerns. The concerns brought to our attention during this year were all valid, and our corrective actions helped solidify our foundation as it related to our goal of changing instruction. Parents were moving past understanding and during the second year were migrating into acceptance.

2011–12 School Year

As we began planning our summer work for the start of the third year using Web 2.0 tools, our focus once again would be on evaluating the existing tools in the toolboxes and making additions, changes, or deletions. In addition, we planned on reviewing the enrollment card information to make sure the verbiage surrounding age-restrictive parental consent was accurate.

Initially, the objective for the third year of Web 2.0 integration was to focus on those teachers who had not yet embraced the new toolset. We now had more teachers using the toolset, which was good, but there were still teachers who, even after two years of coaxing, hadn't started to use the Web 2.0 tools. It was time to lure them in—at least that was our plan going into the summer. However, change was something our district had absolutely embraced, and it was this type of change that would cause us to completely reevaluate our strategy for the third year.

Implementation of the Instructional Coach Model

The district had implemented an instructional coach model for our campuses in the 2010–11 school year. Instructional coaches were designated campus resources specifically focused on helping teachers use data to trend and forecast academic expectations for their students, as well as help with the instructional delivery methods occurring in the classrooms. The model as it existed assigned one coach to multiple campuses.

The cabinet discovered at the end of Year One that the model of multiple campuses sharing one coach wasn't effective. We agreed that if we were going to address instructional delivery seriously in our classrooms, we needed coaches for each core area of curriculum. If we were going to staff the instructional coach model adequately, we needed to significantly increase the number of coaches assigned to the campuses.

As we looked at available staff members in the district who had teaching experience and could successfully fill the role of instructional coach, one group immediately came to the forefront. The members of our Instructional Technology Team had the classroom experience, were familiar with specific curricular areas of focus, and could bring technology integration to the table. The downside? Their work with the initiatives would be dramatically impacted if their numbers were reduced.

As a cabinet, we discussed at great length the pros and cons of changing the makeup of the IT Department. As we reviewed the role of the Instructional Technology Team, we realized that one of the concerns emerging from Year Two was the instructional delivery occurring with teachers using Web 2.0 tools. It didn't make sense to have a group of people focusing on instructional delivery just for those teachers using Web 2.0. Instructional delivery was an issue districtwide, and not only for Web 2.0 classrooms.

Ultimately, we decided to take 22 Instructional Technology Team members and move them into the instructional coach role prior to the start of school. It was a decision that I supported 100 percent, understanding that it was the best decision for our district and its desire to address instructional delivery. However, this decision was difficult for members of the Instructional Technology Team. With this move, their role inside KISD had changed three times in three years. It was very emotional and disruptive for my staff and for the district as a whole. It is important to note that there were approximately 90 new instructional coaching positions to be filled. So, it wasn't just my group being affected by this organizational change. Once again, leadership and communication were going to be the keys as we introduced this organizational change. We needed to have a consistent message and show empathy for those affected, while firmly supporting the decision even when opposition to this organizational change made it to the school board.

The effect on the Instructional Technology Team was huge. The group decreased in size from 26 to four, which immediately affected the speed at which the initiatives and objective for Year Three could be accomplished. The immediate reaction from the group of four was concern over their work on the Web 2.0 implementation initiative. How could four people be expected to do the work of 26? The answer was simple: they couldn't. Instead, we decided that the Instructional Technology Team would now focus solely on the coaches and not on the individual teachers. This made the task much more realistic. Did it slow down the adoption rate? Absolutely. But it did ensure instructional delivery of the Web 2.0 tools was going to occur at the quality level KISD was expecting.

So, the objective for the third year of Web 2.0 implementation changed. Our focus as the Instructional Technology Team would be on educating the instructional coaches and training them on Web 2.0 tools. With this knowledge, the instructional coaches could then take this information back to their campuses and, when appropriate, introduce the toolset to those teachers who had yet to adopt them. More important, the instructional coaches, as they were observing and monitoring instruction, could make any necessary changes for all teachers on their campus who were using Web 2.0 tools. The instructional coaches as a group would spend one day a week meeting with various central administration departments, including the Instructional Technology Team. The coaches' time with my team would be focused on the initiatives.

The Instructional Technology Team members were still conducting "Webinar Wednesday" sessions as well as setting up teacher-led Adobe Connect sessions, so this work from our previous two years did not stop. We were still awarding Digital Star Teacher awards to keep the competitive spirit going. In some cases, Instructional Technology staff members were meeting with campus teachers to provide hands-on training; however, with just four people, this did not occur often.

Once the emotional impact of the organizational change passed, the Instructional Technology Team again focused on the task at hand. To their credit and the credit of their department leader, their work in Year Three was amazing. Department members approached their new focus with the professionalism and excitement expected from staff members working in KISD. The remaining members of the department had a connection to the coaches who had come from our department, which helped facilitate the education process for the coaches who had not yet been exposed to Web 2.0. Not only did this group work with the coaches, they also implemented a new collaboration tool districtwide. In the third year, we rolled out Google Docs to our teachers. This was a great collaboration tool with many additional pieces of functionality. It was one of the most heavily adopted tools in our toolbox and required very little hand holding from the Instructional Technology Team.

Evaluation

As I review Year Three in the Web 2.0 world, it certainly was our most challenging, but I believe it was our most productive. Teachers and students continued to do great work using our toolboxes. We were now focused on instructional delivery occurring at the level KISD was expecting.

The parental issues and concerns from Year Two were not issues in the third year. In this regard, the third year using Web 2.0 was similar to our first. I believe we can attribute this to the fact that in Year Two we paid immediate attention to parents and put in place corrective actions, processes, and procedures to address their concerns. Our parent community not only understood the changes in instruction, they accepted them. It was a great way to conclude our three-year strategic plan and was certainly an initiative we would continue to build on as we determined "What's next?" for KISD as it related to Web 2.0.

CHAPTER 6

Mobile Learning Initiative

My work on the mobile learning initiative started long before KISD decided to incorporate mobile learning into its strategic goal of changing instruction. Once I had defined in my own mind what a mobile learning strategy would look like, I started working on the initiative. I began researching mobile programs at the K–12 level to gain insights about school systems already incorporating mobile learning, particularly those using mobile devices such as smartphones. The research time was pretty quick, simply because in 2009 not many K–12 systems were implementing this radical idea.

As luck would have it, when I attended an Intel gathering for K–12 educators, Elliot Soloway was one of the presenters. Soloway is an Arthur F. Thurnau Professor at the University of Michigan and has appointments in the Department of Electrical Engineering and Computer Science, the College of Engineering, the School of Education, and the School of Information. In my opinion, he is the true pioneer of mobile learning. His presentation specifically addressed mobile phones in the classroom.

Soloway had been doing extensive work overseas in this area, and was discussing the results he had observed with educational systems leveraging these devices. At the conclusion of his presentation I pulled him aside to talk about my ideas regarding mobile learning, the potential impact it could have on education, and my desire to test this approach in KISD. Finally, I had found an educator I could talk to.

My conversations with Soloway were an eye-opening experience. Mobile learning implementation was more complex than I originally thought. In fact, there are so many components to mobile learning beyond the device, it explained why so few K–12 school systems had tried it.

We talked about what age groups should be considered, classroom management software, mobile content, stakeholder acceptance and readiness, parental and school support, technical support both in-house and externally, measurement criteria, and policy impacts. The resulting list of "to-do's" was daunting; however, that did not stop the two of us from formulating an implementation strategy for KISD.

2009–10 School Year

Once mobile learning became an initiative under our district goal, work began immediately. In early March 2009, we defined a pilot project plan with an implementation cycle divided into three phases:

> **Phase 1.** The first phase focused on logistical steps, such as device selection and evaluation of classroom management software, with a completion date of May 31, 2009.

> **Phase 2.** The second phase was tactical preparation of materials, software installation, and hardware configuration, with a completion date of August 31, 2009.

> **Phase 3.** The third and final phase of the initiative was the rollout of these devices to a campus at the start of the 2009 school year.

We knew the idea of giving mobile devices to students was going to be met with resistance and uncertainty from school board members, administrators, teachers, and parents. We needed a rollout strategy that minimized the risks while providing the best opportunities to show the effects mobile devices proved to have on students—good, bad, or neutral.

Phase 1: Logistics

Planning the Pilot Project

Part of KISD's culture as it related to new initiatives was the concept of pilot projects. Pilot projects afford organizations the opportunity to implement new initiatives on a small scale quickly. Pilot projects minimize the risks and allow for more detailed project support. With a small group of users affected by the new initiative, we could easily measure results, compare expected results to actual results, and make any needed course corrections. At the conclusion of the pilot project, fact-based decisions could be made regarding the initiative's success or failure and whether to expand or abandon the project.

Managing risk is at the heart of implementing a pilot model. If the pilot is unsuccessful, it will have affected just a small portion of the end-user community. Also, the financial investment will be significantly lower than for a districtwide rollout.

Our introduction of mobile devices in KISD classrooms would be implemented under this pilot model. To minimize and manage the risk, KISD made the decision to select one campus and one grade level as our pilot participants.

The first logistical order of business when defining our Phase 1 implementation strategy was selecting the grade level we would pilot. Our three-year strategic plan had as one of its objectives the introduction of bring your own device (BYOD) in Year Three. We had to take this into consideration when evaluating our grade level selection.

Based on what I had researched in defining the mobile strategy, a high percentage of secondary students had personal mobile devices that they could use in our BYOD program. However, at the elementary level, personal devices were not nearly as prevalent in 2009. I also found that socioeconomic classification played a significant role when it came to students with personal devices—students from lower economic levels were much less likely to have their own devices.

Soloway shared valuable observations and research data from the mobile learning programs he had been involved with in the United States and abroad. He found that the programs were most successful with fourth through sixth grade students and that this age group showed the highest rate of academic improvement from using these types of devices. Given that our goal in Year Three was to implement a BYOD program and that secondary students were more likely to have their own devices to bring to school than elementary students, we determined that our entry into district-provided mobile devices in the classroom should start at the elementary level.

Once we determined elementary would be our starting point, the next decision was grade level. Again, Soloway provided valuable information based on his experience with these devices in the classroom. At the elementary level, we considered only two grades: fourth graders or fifth graders. Because these would be district-provided devices, we wanted to select the age group that had the highest likelihood from a maturity perspective not only to leverage, but also to respect and have a sense of responsibility for the devices. We decided our pilot with mobile devices in the classroom would occur at a single elementary school for that school's fifth graders.

The Mobile Learning Device (MLD)

One of the points Soloway and I discussed was the perceptions teachers and parents would have of these devices. It was important to refer to the devices in a way that would resonate from an educational perspective. We needed to define a name for these devices that would imply these were tools for learning. We wanted the device name to reflect the educational impact that would result from combining mobile devices with instruction. The term "cell phones" would have a negative connotation, particularly for parents of elementary students. With these criteria in mind and with the advice of Soloway, we determined the devices our fifth graders were going to use would be referred to as *mobile learning devices* (MLDs).

With our project acronym in place, the next logistical task was to identify the MLD that would be used in our pilot project. With our limited budget in mind, I began talking with various carriers about the initiative and what we were hoping to accomplish. Our MLDs had two financial components: cost of the device and the monthly data-plan fee. The budget set aside for the pilot project could not cover the entire cost of both.

As we began conversations with the various carriers, it became clear they were excited about the opportunity to participate in the pilot at KISD. In my discussions with them, I made it known early on that excitement was nice, but if they wanted to participate in our pilot, they would need to risk a little of their own money. I knew if we were successful with our pilot, it would be like the baseball movie *Field of Dreams:* "If you build it, they will come." Mobile learning was coming—all it would take were a few success stories, and mobile learning in the classroom would take off. If a carrier got in on the ground floor, helping to define how mobile learning could be implemented for schools, it would be way ahead of its competitors. KISD was building that foundation, and we wanted more than just vendors—we wanted partners vested in making this pilot a success.

We were able to negotiate a deal with Verizon. Verizon would provide recently discontinued models of devices for free, and KISD would be responsible for the monthly data fee. I will discuss the negotiated monthly fee and the process KISD used later in this chapter. This partnership got us over the first hurdle and allowed the initiative to begin. KISD would receive 130 HTC 6500 Windows Mobile smartphones free of charge, and our monthly data-plan fee would be $38 per device.

In our negotiations with Verizon, we created a plan that turned off cell phone and texting services for all the KISD MLDs. The MLDs would only be able to access the Internet. This was an important configuration setting because the existing district policy banned cell phones in our classrooms. Existing policy also stipulated technology use in the classroom was at the teacher's discretion, so the MLDs would fall under existing policy and would be used at the discretion of the fifth grade teachers. In addition to the policy framework, the configuration settings were important because we did not want these devices to be viewed as cell phones.

Internet Filtering

The other configuration we implemented in partnership with Verizon was the filtering process these MLDs would use when on the Verizon cellular network. Verizon offered Children's Internet Protection Act (CIPA)-compliant filtering for its network; however, we wanted to ensure that the level of filtering was identical to that on our desktop computers. So we worked with Verizon to configure the devices so that when they were on the cellular network, the filtering was actually routed through the KISD filtering systems, not the Verizon filtering systems. The Operations Department spent June and July working with Verizon to establish the filtering process we desired. This was something the Verizon team was confident could happen; the problem was that they had never done it before.

While on paper this seemed like a pretty simple configuration, the reality of making it happen was another. The devices had the option of connecting to any wireless network or connecting to the Verizon cellular network. Our desired configuration was such that if the devices were on the KISD wireless or Verizon cellular network, KISD filtering would be enabled. If the devices were connected to any other wireless network, KISD filtering obviously would not be possible. This would be an issue when students took their devices home to complete homework. We experienced some touch-and-go moments; however, after two months of work our desired configuration was in place and thoroughly tested. We thought that making this configuration change would add a level of comfort for our teachers and the fifth graders' parents.

Enter GoKnow

With the MLD selected, the last logistical item we needed to complete was identifying the classroom management and student tools that teachers would use with the MLDs. Because this was such a new concept for K–12 education, few off-the-shelf software packages specifically focused on mobile devices; in fact, I could not find any. Once again, Soloway was a great resource in this area. Because of his work in mobile learning, he had created a software package specifically focused on mobile devices in the classroom. This software package, called GoKnow, provided classroom management tools, student tools, and professional development tools.

The professional development component of the software package was an unexpected surprise. One of my concerns had been how we would start incorporating these devices into the classroom. The professional development opportunities provided by GoKnow would occur either via onsite meetings or webinars. The webinar component of GoKnow was exciting because it afforded KISD the opportunity to have just-in-time trainings.

Phase 2: Tactical Preparation

We completed our Phase 1 logistical tasks on schedule and turned our attention to Phase 2. As we began working on the tactical Phase 2 components, which would take place over the summer, I realized that proper support of our pilot would require dedicated resources. I took two integration specialists and assigned them full-time as our MLD support team.

Phase 2 tasks that needed to be completed by the MLD team in preparation for the start of school rollout included:

Application Selection

- Determine what software would initially be loaded on the MLDs.

Device Management

- Define management procedures for MLDs.

- Lock the devices to prevent students from changing settings or installing or deleting software.

- Determine the selection criteria for new software.

- Determine the approval process for new software.

- Determine the installation process for new software.

Classroom Management

- Determine how homework would be conveyed to students through their MLDs.

- Determine how students would turn in homework using their MLDs.

- Create training material for teachers.

- Create training material for students.

Lesson Plans, Modeling Strategies, and Wiki

- Develop lesson plans incorporating MLDs.

- Define modeling strategies.

- Create an MLD-specific wiki.

Application Selection

The process of identifying applications to be installed on our MLDs was very quick. The Windows HTC devices came to us with some standard software, enabling word processing, graphics, and spreadsheets. As we started looking for additional software, it struck us how innovative this project really was—there just weren't a lot of applications. Fortunately, because we had partnered with GoKnow, a company with some experience in the mobile world, we were able to benefit from not only GoKnow's software but also its recommendations. Our application list included:

- Sketchy
- Pico Maps
- Go Web
- Go Sync
- Poll Everywhere

- Blogtalk
- WebQuest
- Edublogs
- QR Codes

Device Management

In June 2009, the devices were delivered to KISD. The MLD support team immediately began working on the management procedures that teachers would use. My main concern with the devices was instituting some kind of lockdown process so that students could not change any configuration settings or install or delete software. As the team worked with the devices and Verizon, we were able to configure all of them so that a password was required to make any configuration or software changes. That was the good news; the bad news was if we needed to make a change, it would require touching all 130 devices individually. There was no way to push updates out to the devices automatically. While this was not the optimal solution, the number of devices was small and therefore manageable; it would, however, be a concern should we decide to expand the program beyond one campus.

The last task of device preparation was defining the process for selecting, approving, and installing new applications. This process needed to be thorough, agile, and quick. As we began to define this process there was one nonnegotiable item: any application installed on MLDs in KISD would have to be free. Beyond this point the process was fairly simple. If one of our MLD teachers identified an application he or she felt should be used, the teacher would bring that application to the attention of the MLD fifth grade teaching team (the seven fifth grade teachers). If the team approved, the tool would be reviewed and tested by the Instructional Technology MLD support team. If the support team approved the application, it was installed by the teachers on their devices and tested to make sure it met their instructional expectations. If the application passed the teacher testing, it was then the responsibility of each fifth grade teacher to manually install the application on each student device. With the process defined, our device work was complete. Next on our Phase 2 summer to-do list was the configuration of our classroom management package.

Classroom Management

We selected GoKnow as our partner vendor for the pilot project primarily because of its classroom management software package. Its classroom management application provided the mechanism for teachers to create assignments on their desktop computers and automatically push those assignments out to the students' MLDs. Once the assignment was on the students' devices, students would complete their homework and submit it. The homework was then reviewed and graded from the teacher's computer.

With staff from GoKnow, the MLD support team worked for two months during the summer, testing and documenting the process from a teacher's perspective as well as a student's perspective. The time spent learning the new system also provided the foundation from which all of our teacher and student training materials were created. It was a very intuitive system and key to our rollout. We would not have to spend a lot of time on the "system" side of this pilot. The majority of time could be focused on incorporating devices into the classroom, which is what we wanted.

Lesson Plans, Modeling Strategies, and Wiki

The last bit of tactical work to be completed in the summer was creating lesson plans, modeling strategies, and a wiki. The MLD support team worked with the GoKnow team, and we jointly examined our curriculum scope and sequence for the first six weeks of the school year. We developed some lesson plans and modeling strategies that would incorporate the MLDs. Having a resource familiar with the mobile world expedited our preparation time in these areas.

During the process of creating lessons plans, the team decided to create an MLD-specific wiki. While we had a districtwide knowledgebase, the team felt we needed to create a one-stop shopping location for this pilot project. The wiki would provide a location for all of our training material, FAQs, sample lessons, sample modeling strategies, and application overviews. It would be a place where the teachers could come together online and collaborate. They could post questions, solutions, and samples. For the pilot project, we didn't expect communication to be an issue, given we were just using one campus and a small group of teachers. But if and when we decided to roll this out beyond one campus, having a wiki space with this content and opportunities for teacher input would be invaluable. As the team developed lessons for the first six weeks, they uploaded them into the new wiki. And with that, the summer of 2009 quickly came to a close. We were ready to roll out the pilot project!

Selecting the Pilot Campus

The one unanswered question in our rollout plan was which school would be our pilot campus. We needed to select a campus that had a strong technology culture and was forward thinking. It needed an area superintendent and a principal willing to support this pilot initiative 100 percent. They would need to be the primary champions of the initiative and spearhead the implementation. Success for the pilot project would be dependent on them. Furthermore, the principal would need to have a solid relationship with the parent community as this person would be the face of the initiative for the parents.

We needed to select a campus that had a strong fifth grade teaching team. This team needed to have a culture and mindset that embraced technology and innovation with a high percentage of teachers already taking advantage of Web 2.0 toolboxes. We were fortunate in KISD to have a number of elementary campuses that met our criteria—always a nice problem to have when deciding to embark on something so different.

Throughout the formalization of my mobile learning strategy, I had been bouncing ideas off one of KISD's area superintendents, Joe Kelley, introduced in Chapter 3. Kelley was my main sounding board when it came to formalizing the mobile strategy. He had been a high school principal and seen firsthand the impact "powering down" had on his students as they entered his building. Linking Kelley into this initiative as the area superintendent champion was an obvious choice, since he had been with me throughout my entire journey and supported this initiative.

In early June 2009, Joe and I selected the elementary campus we thought would be perfect for piloting our mobile initiative. Mindy Dickerson was the campus principal at Cimarron Elementary, and her school was our choice for the pilot. The campus had seven fifth grade teachers and 130 fifth grade students. We met her with our selling hats in hand, ready to do whatever it took to get her to decide to take on this pilot project.

To our surprise, the conversation took about 10 minutes. Dickerson was very much a forward-thinking campus leader, one who embraced technology and made sure integration was occurring on her campus. She was one of those principals always looking for better ways to provide learning opportunities for teachers and students. She had a great relationship with her teachers as well as her parent community and was not only willing, but excited to pilot this initiative.

With the leadership component of the pilot solidified, we were ready to start the introduction process to the fifth grade teaching team (six general education teachers and one special education teacher). The benefit of having strong district and campus leadership on the team was that they were ready to take ownership of the initiative as it related to not only the implementation, but any campus and class-room management issues that these devices might introduce.

Working with Kelley and Dickerson, we created the introduction and implementation presentation for the fifth grade teaching team. Our plan was to introduce the initiative and the campus's role in the pilot project and then to immediately put the devices into the teachers' hands. We wanted to give the teachers ample time to familiarize themselves with the devices before starting any formal professional development. We decided to time our introductory meeting for the first week after teachers returned from their summer breaks.

Introducing the Pilot Project

We had two goals for the MLD introduction meeting. We wanted to both clearly articulate what it meant to be a pilot campus and get the MLDs into the teachers' hands.

To meet our first goal, at the introductory meeting we explained the roles and responsibilities as well as expectations associated with being a "pilot." We wanted this group of fifth grade teachers to understand that we would all be in unchartered waters. We were creating something from scratch, and in doing so, there would be bumps along the way. It was their role as a pilot campus to discover and work through all the bumps, chart the course others would follow, and stay positive with their students and parents.

To meet our second goal for this meeting, we just needed to get the actual MLDs into these teachers' hands. We gave the teachers a brief overview of how to use the device, then told them to spend some time familiarizing themselves with the devices, and asked them to think about the pilot project. We didn't want to overload the teachers in this meeting with a lot of sample lesson plans or start the process of modeling instruction. They were in enough shock! We wanted to give them time to "play" with the device and just get familiar with how it worked. We reassured them that additional meetings would be scheduled in a few weeks to talk about starting the pilot project in their classes. They would have an opportunity at that meeting to ask any questions or voice any concerns.

I wish you could have seen the looks on all of their faces at the beginning of this meeting. It varied from total disbelief, to complete fear, to "You're joking"—and then the wheels started turning. Having the area superintendent and principal take the lead in this portion of the discussion made the process go smoothly. They had the "street cred," so to speak, to confidently answer all the teachers' questions and reassure them that the mobile learning initiative was going to be a good thing.

Some of the concerns voiced by the teachers involved classroom management and discipline. The teachers would face not only the challenge of integration, but also changes in the management dynamics within their classrooms. In addition, the MLDs would introduce new discipline issues that teachers and administrators had not dealt with previously. Addressing these concerns was an opportunity to review with these teachers the pilot concept. These were all valid questions, and problems would undoubtedly occur at some point in our pilot year. We didn't have all the answers, but when these opportunities presented themselves, we would work through them together. I won't say that all seven teachers came on board immediately, but they weren't running out of the conference room screaming.

And that was it. The introduction meeting was done. We had met our two goals. The principal showed confidence and commitment to the pilot. No teacher had objected to the concept or pilot. All in all, we considered the first meeting a huge success. The summer was over, and a new school year was upon us.

Phase 3: Rollout

The 2009–10 school year began, and with it, so did our MLD pilot rollout schedule. Certain events in the schedule needed to occur in specific sequences, so we needed the MLD participants to understand the rollout schedule and begin their communication process. We first needed to establish the date students would receive the MLDs and set dates backward from there. We needed to schedule teacher training so that they would be ready to incorporate the MLDs into their curriculum, and we needed to schedule a parent meeting and obtain parental approvals.

Teacher Training

Work began almost immediately on teacher training. The easy part of the training was instructing teachers on how to use the GoKnow management software package. The software was intuitive so we didn't have to spend a lot of time on it. The majority of our training effort was getting the fifth grade team comfortable with integrating these devices into their classrooms. To assist them, we had worked all summer developing lesson plans incorporating the devices that could be used for the first six weeks of school.

The biggest issue we had during this phase of the training was not getting teachers to use the lessons plans we developed, but getting them to think differently about their personal delivery methods. Even among the seven teachers on our fifth grade team, teaching styles varied greatly.

The teachers also had various levels of comfort when it came to using the MLDs. Providing the lessons plans diminished their apprehension, but it didn't go away completely. Their greatest apprehension centered around the role they would play in developing new lessons beyond what we had provided. Luckily, developing new lesson plans wasn't completely on the shoulders of the fifth grade teachers. The MLD support team as well as the GoKnow team would continue to develop lessons as well. As the fifth grade teachers became more comfortable with the MLDs, they also became more comfortable developing lesson plans using the devices, and created more and more lesson plans.

As we were developing the lessons, we needed to consider that some students in the class might not receive parental consent, would lose their devices, or because of disciplinary actions not be allowed to use their MLDs. What would teachers do for that subset of students? They needed to have something prepared that was engaging without the MLDs. When those situations did occur we found the teachers relied on lessons plans used pre-MLD. This proved to be a great resource for two reasons. First, it saved time for the teachers because they did not have to create two lesson plans for each lesson. They could rely on the veteran teachers to provide the more traditional plans. Second, this was an effective disincentive for students. They did not like going back to the "paper and pencil" work when all their classmates were using their MLDs.

Parent Night

Now that our fifth grade teachers had the devices and were familiarizing themselves with them, we turned our attention to parent night.

We carefully planned our agenda. We knew parental buy-in would make or break this initiative. If we could not get the parents excited and willing to try the mobile learning initiative, our pilot would never get off the ground.

The first challenge was making sure the meeting was well attended, something that is very difficult, particularly at the start of a new school year. The parent meeting was scheduled and notifications/invitations were sent home. Principal Dickerson did a good job of enticing her fifth grade parents, because a high percentage of parents attended. The most effective thing she did to achieve this was to tie students' getting their devices to their parents' attendance. She spent a lot of time with the students in the days leading up to the meeting, telling them how important it was for their parents to show up. She also sent home communications with the students and utilized the district's automated call system to reach every home and let parents know their children would not receive the device if they didn't attend.

Dickerson started off the meeting talking about the pilot process for implementing projects in KISD. She talked about why she volunteered and why she thought this mobile learning initiative was worthwhile. She talked about the KISD curriculum and how these devices would enhance learning, not detract from it.

The parents needed to understand that they and their children were charting the course that would benefit future students and teachers. They needed to understand there would be bumps along the way. There would be surprises and issues. But with their support and help, we would work through obstacles, making it that much easier for the next campus.

Once Dickerson had explained the pilot concept, I introduced the project and device. I demonstrated the device, spending time discussing functionality and focusing on security, data protection, and web filtering. Parents needed to understand these devices would be coming home with their children and were going to be used in the process of completing homework assignments.

When the devices were on the KISD wireless or Verizon cellular networks, they were being filtered. However, these devices could connect to any wireless network. Parents needed to understand that reality and accept some responsibility as it related to when and how the devices were being used outside the school walls.

The meeting ended with a question-and-answer session. We valued and wanted the parents' input, suggestions, and concerns. We wanted them to understand that they could not be silent partners in this project. We gave the parents the opportunity to ask as many questions as they wanted in order to become comfortable with this initiative. Our goal for the evening was for all parents to sign the MLD consent forms allowing their children to accept the MLDs and use them in the classroom.

The majority of parental questions or concerns focused on two things: curriculum and safety. From a curriculum perspective, parents wanted to ensure their children were learning from the standards-based curriculum just like the fifth graders who weren't using MLDs. They didn't want a specific MLD curriculum that was being developing and "tested" on their students. In fact, this is a question that came up at every parent meeting for all three years. We reassured parents that there is only one curriculum in KISD, not separate MLD and non-MLD curriculums. We informed them that we had worked for the past two months to identify integration opportunities within the curriculum for MLDs. We told the parents that MLDs were not replacing traditional instruction. There was a time and place for paper-and-pencil learning, and there was a time and place for MLDs.

Security questions varied from identity management to Internet safety. I told parents the devices contained no personal information related to their children, so if an MLD were lost, their children's personal information would not be at risk. I discussed our filtering solution, specifically focusing on the fact that these devices could connect to any wireless network. I asked them how many had wireless networks at home; just about every hand went up. I reiterated that filtering was in place for the KISD wireless and Verizon networks; however, if their child got onto their home wireless network or the one at Starbucks, those networks may not be filtered, and the children would have the ability to get to any website they chose. I wanted the parents to understand that KISD was doing everything it could, but they also had to understand they had a role in their children having these devices and parental monitoring was still necessary.

I also received questions about lost or broken devices. I told the parents they were not financially responsible for lost or broken devices. I didn't want the financial part of the project to scare parents away. Although there was not a financial obligation if devices were lost or broken, there would be some kind of replacement process the student would have to go through to get a new device.

The most interesting question out of the whole night was this: "So, my child gets this as a fifth grader; does he take this to sixth grade? If he doesn't, why do this at all if it will just benefit them for one year?" In all our prep meetings talking about potential questions, this one never bubbled up and we had never considered this issue. It was a valid question and allowed me the opportunity to revisit with this group of parents the foundation of our strategic goal: it is not about the device, it is about gradually changing all instruction.

The devices would not follow their children to sixth grade. However, this instructional change was occurring districtwide. Even though a child might not have an MLD, he or she would have access to Web 2.0 tools, interactive whiteboards, and other tech tools—all enablers of instructional change. With each passing year, this change would become more and more institutionalized, we explained. What their children would learn that year with the devices would be leveraged the following year and throughout all their educational experiences at KISD.

The parent meeting lasted about two-and-a-half hours. We did not leave until every parent had an opportunity to ask questions or voice concerns. At the end of the evening, we had signed consent forms from every parent in attendance. We were ready to give the devices to the students.

Putting the Devices into Students' Hands

As expected, rolling out these devices to students was amazing! The students were excited when they learned the devices would actually go home with them. Their ability to pick up these devices and immediately start working on them reinforced to all of us that this tool could have significant impact. We didn't spend time training them how to use the device—we spent training time on the care and upkeep of these devices, covering things like charging, transporting, storage, and responsible use.

The students were instructed to charge their MLDs at night. If they came to school with a dead MLD, they would not be allowed to charge it there. I won't spend a lot of time talking about the student training because it was a minor part of the rollout. Instead, I will highlight the results and issues we experienced in our pilot year with MLDs.

Results

Teacher Observations

Because of using the MLDs in the classroom, the teachers observed:

- immediate and sustained improvement in engagement
- increased time on task
- higher-level cognitive skills
- creativity
- collaboration
- changes in classroom dynamics

Of the total time in class spent on science, math, reading, language, and social studies, over 50% was spent on activities involving MLDs.

The rest of the time was spent on traditional paper and pencil activities or activities that didn't require the use of MLDs. I was encouraged by this utilization percentage for the program. Given what I was seeing with the adoption of Web 2.0 tools, my expectation was much less in the first year of incorporating MLDs into the classrooms.

Immediate and sustained improved engagement. Engagement was instant once the devices were incorporated into the instructional process. Using the devices, students were truly interested in the work. Whether it was looking up words, working on math problems, or animating the water cycle, students were engaged. The devices created an environment in which the students wanted to learn.

Increased time on task. This was a particularly interesting finding. One of the biggest concerns for the teachers when we introduced this concept was that these devices would distract students from their work. I think all the teachers going into the school year believed their biggest challenge would be getting the students to do what they wanted them to when they wanted them to do it.

The fifth grade teachers were amazed to discover that this was not an issue—one of their happiest surprises. The MLDs were not a distraction—in fact, they were the hook that got the students' attention and kept their focus on whatever the task was. Because the students were engaged at such a deep level, the teachers weren't spending a lot of time getting students back on task. In fact, the comments from our teachers were just the opposite—they had a difficult time getting the students to move on to something else. Wow, what a great problem to have!

This is not to say that classroom management wasn't an issue. I just want to make the point that introducing these devices did not add another level of complexity to classroom management. Whether the devices were used or not, teachers still had to manage their classrooms.

Higher-level cognitive skills. Teacher feedback in this area focused on the quality of homework being turned in by their students using the MLDs. In the typical paper-and-pencil classroom, a few students would consistently excel when it came to homework assignments. Our fifth grade teachers discovered a higher number of their students were turning in homework above and beyond the requirements.

The work being turned in by the MLD students for their general homework assignments was at skill and knowledge levels typically seen for extra credit work. This was an exciting finding because it dovetailed with increased engagement and time on task. When the students were engaged and on task, they were willing to spend more time on homework. Teachers found that most students didn't even realize they were spending more time—all they knew was that, for the first time, homework could be fun.

Creativity. Teachers commented on how the devices brought out the students' individual personalities and creativity. They were amazed at some of the work being produced on the devices by students they wouldn't have expected it from. The consistent observation regarding creativity was that teachers would never have seen some of the personality traits or creativity had the students been using only the traditional paper-and-pencil model.

Collaboration. The MLDs enabled collaboration, something I witnessed along with the teachers. I was observing a science lesson that had two classrooms combined into one room—lots of students in a small space with lots of noise. I remember thinking, "Holy cow, this is way too noisy. How can they get anything accomplished?" The teacher explained to me that the students were divided into teams of four. Each team was assigned an imaginary planet and had to define the climate, food, clothing, and entertainment their planet would offer and then come up with a commercial to attract people to their planet. Each member took on one of the four components, and they would sync each component with the other members of the team using their MLDs. When I got close to each table, I was amazed listening to the conversations occurring. Each student was using the MLD to complete the component they were responsible for, yet within each group of four emerged a leader, a detail taskmaster, a creative contributor, and so on. I observed with these fifth grade groups all the roles we see emerge in adult groups.

Changes in classroom dynamics. Our fifth grade teachers talked about how their roles had changed. No longer were they just in front of their classes lecturing in the typical "sit-and-get" mode. The dynamics of the classroom changed because the teacher was no longer the expert on everything. Students were taking leadership roles in regard to the MLDs and what could be accomplished using them. In some cases, teachers would let their students lead portions of the lesson. Students were now in front of the class, talking about things they discovered their MLDs could do. More important, the students in front of the class talking about the devices were not the students typically willing to get up and speak.

We compared discipline records for these fifth graders to their records from fourth grade and noted that discipline issues had decreased. We also compared attendance records for these fifth graders to their fourth grade records and found that attendance had gone up.

We lost one device the entire year, and you will laugh at the excuse brought to the campus by the student. It was, "The dog ate my MLD." Even as we transform and progress into the digital era, that same excuse we used as children is still plausible!

Parental Support

Support from parents of fifth graders was incredible. They were communicative and very demanding. They pushed us and yet were willing to compromise when trying to resolve issues. They took active roles in the lives of their children related to these devices. We knew this was a critical group if the pilot were going to be successful, and we could not have asked for a better pilot parent community.

Benchmark Scores

The real measurement for our pilot was evaluating benchmark scores. Benchmark tests are given by the district to measure student progress in core classes at each grade level. The tests are administered each semester. Table 6.1 shows the average benchmark scores of the group of students who were in the pilot group, from fourth grade (traditional instruction) to fifth grade (use of the MLDs).

TABLE 6.1   Average scores for students in the pilot group who received traditional instruction in fourth grade (2009) and received instruction using the MLDs in fifth grade (2010)

Subject	Average Scores Fourth Grade (2009) (traditional instruction)	Average Scores Fifth Grade (2010) (instruction using MLDs)
Reading	86	94
Math	80	92
Science	NA*	95

* Not applicable. There is no benchmark test for fourth grade science.

Table 6.2 compares the average scores of all fifth grade students in the district from 2009 (traditional instruction) to the fifth graders in the pilot group who were using the MLDs in 2010.

TABLE 6.2   Average scores for fifth graders receiving traditional instruction (in 2009) and using the MLDs (in 2010)

Subject	Average Scores District Fifth Graders (2009) (traditional instruction)	Average Scores Pilot Group Fifth Graders (2010) (instruction using MLDs)
Reading	94	94
Math	89	92
Science	87	95

As you can see, the results are pretty amazing. Can we attribute all of the increases to our change of instruction and the integration of MLDs? The answer is no. However, if you evaluate what changed in the area of instruction for the fifth grade class, MLDs were a significant component in the change equation. Therefore, their role in the dramatic improvement cannot be minimized.

Issues

The results of the pilot program were overwhelmingly positive. However, we needed to evaluate the issues to make a decision regarding continuing, expanding, or abandoning this initiative.

Finances

Let's start with the financial component of this initiative. There are two funding elements to be considered regarding the MLDs: the device cost and monthly data fee. We also utilized two funding sources: district funds and E-Rate funds.

Concerning the device cost, E-Rate rules clearly state this money cannot be used to purchase this type of device. Funding for devices, if required for subsequent years, would be the responsibility of KISD.

Regarding the monthly data fee, this is a much more complicated scenario. If you recall from Chapter 1, E-Rate rules state that E-Rate money can be used to pay for service provider data plan fees but only while the devices are on district facilities. This presented a problem for KISD. While the devices were on our district facilities (i.e., on a campus) they were connected to KISD's internal Wi-Fi network instead of the Verizon network and, as a result, E-Rate funding could not be utilized. It is important to note that changes in the E-Rate rules, especially regarding student devices and data plan fees, were being discussed at this time. KISD applied each year for funding in hopes that the rules would soon change and we would be able leverage E-Rate funds for our MLD program.

So the bottom line for funding the MLD program beyond Year One was simple: unless the E-Rate rules changed regarding student devices and data plan fees, the program would need to be funded 100% by KISD. With data plans roughly $38 per month per device in addition to the device cost, our initiative could be very expensive to expand beyond a single campus.

Device

As we evaluated the HTC 6500 Windows Mobile device during our pilot year, we identified a few functional issues. Now, don't get me wrong—we understood these devices were free, and we were extremely grateful. However, if we were going to expand beyond the pilot campus, the issues identified in our pilot year needed to be addressed.

The first issue was the ability these devices had to connect to any Wi-Fi network within range. Our preference—especially if our numbers increased significantly—would be to have devices that we could lock down to limit Wi-Fi network connections. While we did not experience problems with this during our pilot year, we felt allowing MLDs to connect with other Wi-Fi networks could become problematic.

The second issue was device management. When we had 130 devices, manual support and intervention were acceptable. If we were to expand beyond that number, support of these devices would require some type of automated process for configuration and software installation.

Third, these devices did not support Flash. This proved to be problematic for a number of the resources and websites that teachers were hoping to use with the MLDs. This was the highest ranked issue as defined by the teachers.

Resources

Availability of mobile-enabled educational resources was very limited. We knew this going into the pilot year and hoped that our partnership with GoKnow would compensate for the shortage.

While the relationship with GoKnow added tremendous value in the early phases of our pilot project, our fifth grade teaching team had leveraged the educational resources provided by GoKnow within the first two months and were struggling to find new resources to keep their students engaged and challenged. While the GoKnow team was willing to assist in finding new resources, the classroom teachers were much closer to the actual work and were much more active in trying to identify new resources beyond the initial implementation. This meant the KISD team members, within a couple of months, were essentially on their own. As you could see from the exciting results, this reality didn't compromise the initiative. However, the limited number of mobile resources was a concern.

Classroom Management and Discipline

Finally, we evaluated the impact these devices had on classroom management and discipline. While the devices did change the dynamics within classrooms, the responsibility of classroom management fundamentally didn't change. If teachers just sat at their desks, whether the students had devices or not, they were going to experience classroom management issues.

From a discipline perspective, the fifth grade teaching team did encounter some inappropriate behavior when students used the devices and implemented appropriate consequences. Depending on the severity, discipline ranged from removal of the device for a specified period of time up to removal of the device and a parent meeting. Regardless of the disciplinary issue, a corrective action was identified that the student had to complete before being reissued the MLD. The MLDs introduced new disciplinary scenarios; however, the team felt it had established solid processes and procedures to address each case.

Outcome of Pilot Project

Based on the results and issues identified, did we achieve the expected outcome? Did the introduction of MLDs into the classrooms enable our fifth grade teaching team to change instruction fundamentally?

While the issues identified above did present certain challenges, particularly from a funding perspective, it was a unanimous decision to declare this pilot a success and recommend the project not only be continued, but expanded, for the 2010–11 school year.

2010–11 School Year

We began planning for our second-year expansion in May 2010. Through that planning process, we identified seven action items that needed to be completed over the summer before the rollout at the beginning of the school year. As we worked through the action items, we found another action item (item 3) needed to be added to the list. Here are those action items:

1. Determine the scope of expansion.
2. Select and configure the MLDs.
3. Select a classroom management system.
4. Automate software installation.
5. Identify pre-installed applications.
6. Update training materials.
7. Notify expansion campus principals.

Just like in our pilot year, we divided the implementation into three phases.

Phase 1: Logistics. The first phase focused on logistical steps such as determining which additional campuses would get MLDs and selecting the device, with a completion date of May 31, 2010.

Phase 2: Tactical Preparation. The second phase included tactical steps such as selecting a classroom management system, preparing the MLD budget, automating software installation, updating training materials, configuring hardware, and notifying the principals at expansion campuses, with a completion date of August 31, 2010.

Phase 3: Rollout. The final phase would be the actual rollout of the devices to a campus at the beginning of the 2010 school year.

Phase 1. Logistics

As we began planning for Phase 1 action items, I realized much of the work was already complete, thanks to our decision to file for E-Rate funding for the MLD program for the 2010–11 school year.

The application for funding was due in February 2010 (the second semester of our pilot year). Although no changes had been made to the E-Rate rules regarding mobile devices and limitations set forth regarding service provider data plan fees, conversations were still occurring at the FCC level that gave me hope changes were on the way. Because there was a strong indication of possible policy changes, I decided to go ahead and apply for E-Rate money specifically focused on our MLD program and associated service provider data plan fees. There was no risk in applying because expansion of our program was not going to be dependent on any decisions the FCC might or might not make.

A requirement of E-Rate is that any expense for which you are expecting to use E-Rate money must be approved through a formal request for proposal (RFP) process. For us to create an RFP to find wireless carrier plans, we needed to finalize the scope and scale of our expansion—in other words, we needed to know the number of campuses and the total number of devices.

Determine the Scope of Expansion

Given that there was a tremendous amount of uncertainty regarding public education funding and, barring an E-Rate policy change, all of the funding for our expansion was coming solely from KISD, a districtwide rollout to all elementary campuses was not going to be possible. We could expand only to a subset of our elementary schools. Our challenge was determining which schools would become our expansion campuses.

My goal was to maximize reimbursement in the event of an E-Rate policy change. That meant selecting those campuses with the highest E-Rate reimbursement percentages. As I evaluated our elementary campuses, I found we had 10 schools that were at KISD's highest reimbursable rate of 80 percent. Given that the district would be responsible for all the funding should no E-Rate policy changes occur, expansion to these 10 schools was reviewed by the CFO's office and deemed financially viable. Our scope and scale for Year Two E-Rate was defined at 11 elementary campuses. Our RFP for MLD data plans covering fifth grade classrooms on 11 campuses—our pilot school plus the 10 additional 80 percent campuses, which equated to roughly 1,700 devices—was completed in November of 2009.

Before reviewing any RFP responses, I had been hoping that wireless carriers were starting to see the light when it came to education and mobile learning. If carriers could develop education data plans that moved the price point from $38 per month per device down to $10 per month per device, schools would stand in line to sign up. Sadly, after I reviewed the responses to the RFP, I concluded that carriers had not bought into the concept of mobile learning in education. While we were able to negotiate a slightly lower data plan fee compared to the first year, it wasn't nearly low enough to allow us to increase the scale of our expansion. We selected Verizon once again with a data plan rate of $35 per month.

With the RFP process complete and our expansion campuses identified, we submitted the appropriate E-Rate paperwork. Completing our E-Rate filing also meant we completed the first action item on our implementation list. We also completed half of the second action item. We had identified the vendor—all that remained was selecting the device itself.

Select and Configure the MLDs

We knew the world of smartphones was dynamic and evolving quickly, and we wanted to take advantage of any advances in the capabilities of MLDs. We took the list of device issues from the first year (device management, ability to limit network access, ability to support Flash) and used that as a starting point for our new evaluation criteria. Also, at a minimum we required devices with cameras, video recording abilities, and availability of a wider range of applications.

Once we established our criteria, we worked with Verizon to begin the evaluation process. Very quickly our focus turned toward the Android suite of devices. The feature sets of the Android devices were much broader than for our first-year Windows Mobile device. And the availability of potentially useful applications was exponentially higher in the Android market.

The downside to the Android operating system was that GoKnow, our classroom management system, did not have an Android version. The company was developing it but was not sure if the new version would be ready for the start of the 2010–11 school year. This caused a problem in our device evaluation process. If we stayed with the Windows devices, we knew most of the issues identified in our Year One pilot project would not be addressed. However, we would have the benefit of using the same classroom management suite. If we moved to the Android operating system, the functional issues from Year One would be addressed. However, we would be forced to select a new classroom management software package.

We went back to the pilot campus teachers and talked with them. Given a choice, their overwhelming preference was for the Android devices with more functionality and greater availability of useful applications.

Working with Verizon, we selected the HTC Android Incredible smartphone as our Year Two MLD. The phone and texting services would be turned off for the smartphones, just like on our pilot devices. These new devices had Flash functionality, which was the highest ranked issue identified by our pilot campus. Additionally, these new devices had a configuration setting specifying the wireless networks they could connect to. Remember, our pilot devices could connect to any wireless network in range, which was one of our biggest concerns when considering expansion. We configured the new devices so that only two wireless networks would be available to them, the KISD wireless and Verizon cellular. Both of these networks were routed through our filtering system as in Year One.

The last device-specific task was selecting protective cases for these devices. These new devices were more fragile than those used in our pilot year, and we would now have to pay for replacement units so we needed something fairly sturdy. We decided to go with low cost, mid-quality protective cases, hoping they would be sufficient for the new devices.

We were right on schedule. It was the end of May 2010, and we were ready for our Phase 2 action items.

Phase 2. Tactical Preparation

Select a Classroom Management Tool

Because we selected the Android MLD, we had to add a new action item to our Phase 2 list: selecting a classroom management system. Sometimes in life things just fall into place without your even having to think about them. That was the case for us related to selecting a new MLD classroom management software package.

As luck would have it, the district had been experimenting with Edmodo, a Web 2.0 classroom management tool. The Instructional Technology Team members who were familiar with this tool were impressed with its flexibility, multiple levels of functionality, and ease of use. The classroom teachers using it liked the collaboration it enabled between them and their students. Parents liked the tool because it had a parent access view, allowing them to see homework assignments from the teacher and their children.

As we began having meetings regarding an MLD classroom management package, Edmodo quickly came to the top of everyone's list. It had functionality similar to our previous classroom management software. More important, it was intuitive and easy to use, so training was not going to be a big issue. The other nice thing about this tool was it could be used in any classroom in KISD; the process was virtually the same for regular classrooms and MLD classrooms. For those of you unfamiliar with Edmodo, I highly recommend this Web 2.0 tool. We have had great success using Edmodo, so much so that it has become the standard classroom management tool for all our K–12 classrooms.

Automate Software Installation

The software installation process was the next action item. Managing this process was a major concern that emerged from our pilot year as we considered expansion. We needed to have an automated installation process such that if a new software package was selected, installation could be done automatically for each device, requiring no manual intervention.

With the selection of the Android device, we were pleasantly surprised as we began defining the installation process. First, the student MLD would not have the ability to connect to the application market, eliminating the possibility of students installing applications. Second, we were able to create a master Google account that was associated with all of the devices. The master Google account was given to each of the teachers. Teachers had the ability, using their MLDs, to get to the application market (now called Google Play) and if approved, use this master Google account to push the selected application to all of their students' devices. This was much easier than manually installing applications, especially when you consider we would have 1,700 MLDs for Year Two.

Identify Pre-Installed Applications

Next for Phase 2, our MLD team began identifying applications that would come pre-installed on the devices. Just like in the pilot year, our preference was to select free applications, and to date we have been very successful in maintaining this philosophy.

Much to our delight, the number of educational applications had dramatically increased compared to Year One. The Android market offered a wider variety of educational applications than Windows Mobile. We also saw a significant increase in mobile applications from our educational vendors. Maybe the cellular companies hadn't bought into this mobile concept, but the educational vendors certainly had. We were able to identify appropriate applications for each content area. For a list of our content-specific MLD applications for language arts, science, social studies, and references, see Appendix A.

Update Training Materials

Updating and modifying our training materials to support the new device and classroom management software was next on our action item list. I was concerned that switching our device would render all our lesson plans and modeling documents worthless for Year Two. Luckily, the existing documentation required only minor tweaks. This was a helpful timesaver because we had identified a number of new applications for which we needed to develop lesson plans and modeling sessions.

Because of our decision to go with the Android device, our implementation partner from the pilot year, GoKnow, was no longer an option, which meant the MLD team was on its own for Year Two. We needed to spend our time very wisely. Because of this, we focused on developing lesson plans using the new applications for the first three weeks of school, instead of six weeks as we had done for the pilot project. We narrowed the time frame considerably, with the expectation that our pilot teachers and some of the new teachers would assist in developing lesson plans beyond the first three weeks. At a minimum, we could use the existing lesson plans and modeling sessions from our pilot year to cover any gaps.

We also spent time updating our MLD wiki and knowledgebase. This was important given that we still had only two Instructional Technology Team members dedicated to the MLD program, but we were introducing a number of new applications and were expanding the user base by 10 campuses. We needed to make sure all support alternatives were up-to-date if we were going to be successful in supporting this new group of users. We planned on making use of the Adobe Connect functionality as part of our support structure. We could quickly get the fifth grade teachers together virtually and go over any questions and concerns or simply encourage them to talk among themselves. We were hoping to leverage our pilot campus teachers by having them conduct Connect sessions with our new campuses and model the use of the MLDs in an upcoming lesson plan just like we did with the Web 2.0 tools.

Notify Expansion Campus Principals

The last step in Phase 2 was introducing the proposed implementation schedule to our new group of expansion principals and answering any of their questions. The nice thing about planning for this meeting was all of the expansion principals were familiar with the MLD pilot and were excited that the program was coming to their campuses.

Our pilot project principal, Mindy Dickerson, kicked off the introduction meeting, talking about her experience with MLDs on her campus. She spent a lot of time describing what she did as the campus leader to ensure the integration of the devices was not only occurring, but occurring in a manner that truly enhanced student engagement and facilitated improved student achievement. She talked about the varying degrees of comfort with the devices among her team, saying that each teacher had to embrace the device on his or her own terms. While she allowed flexibility and time for the teachers to embrace the devices, she didn't allow a teacher to simply "walk away" from the initiative. She clarified the role of principal for our expansion campuses and set me up perfectly to talk about the proposed implementation schedule and next steps.

I walked the principals through the five rollout implementation steps, explaining each step and the various support mechanisms in place along the rollout implementation cycle. The implementation steps and their timing are as follow:

1. Teachers receive MLDs. (Two weeks before formal training)
2. Teacher training takes place. (Days 1 and 2)
3. Parent meeting is held. (Day 3)
4. Devices are distributed to students. (Day 4)
5. Students are taught their first lesson with the MLDs. (Day 5)

I wanted the principals to understand that their role in the MLD project was not tactical or logistical. The MLD support team would provide that. Their role for the MLD project was providing instructional leadership. I wanted the principals to walk away from the meeting with a sense of comfort, clearly understanding their role and the role of our MLD support team and how together we would make the project a success on their campuses. This was not an initiative they could turn over to the MLD support team and assume the results seen at our pilot campus were going to be realized on theirs.

I talked about the process we were going to use to introduce their teachers to the device. Like we did with the pilot campus, we were planning on giving the expansion teachers the devices when they first came back from vacation. The teachers would have the devices for a couple of weeks before any formal training occurred. The challenge we had was scheduling the training for this pool of teachers. I wanted principals' feedback on feasible options for training their fifth grade teachers on the MLDs. They had plenty of time to consider this, but it was something we were very concerned about.

We then opened up the meeting for questions. The questions varied, depending on the technical comfort level of each principal. It was a great opportunity for our MLD support team to get a clear picture of what kind of culture existed at each of our expansion campuses. The fact that each campus had its unique culture was never more evident than during our Q&A session. Some principals were champing at the bit to be first on the implementation path. Some principals wanted to see detailed schedules and timelines. And a few principals wanted to sit back, let their peers jump into this, and then follow along after. We also had principals at bilingual campuses who were concerned about language barriers at the parent meeting. By being alerted to this issue early, we were able to arrange for presentations by bilingual teachers at these meetings.

I considered the principals' meeting to be a success—we didn't have anyone decline from the expansion pool, and as a whole, the group was excited about the opportunity.

The last order of business for our principal meeting was to discuss rollout options. We wanted to have all 11 campuses using the devices with their students by November 1, 2010. To meet this date, we planned for two campus rollouts per week. We wanted the principals to pencil in the week they would like to have the devices rolled out on their campuses. Once we had this schedule we could then define parent night meetings and teacher training sessions.

With that, Phase 2 was complete, and we were at the end of the summer and ready for the implementation.

Phase 3. Rollout

Teachers Receive MLDs

We scheduled one meeting for all 11 of our fifth grade teaching teams. The rollout of our MLDs to the teachers was a very interesting meeting. As was the case with the principals, everyone at the meeting was aware of the pilot from the previous year, but most teachers from our 10 new campuses had very little understanding beyond "kids in fifth grade get devices." I was surprised by this lack of knowledge about the pilot and what our MLD teachers were doing with the devices and their students.

During the meeting, we spent time talking about the MLD pilot and the results we had seen. Some of the pilot campus teachers came to the meeting and talked about their experiences. They talked about their concerns going into the pilot and how those concerns played out throughout the implementation. They talked about the effects that devices had on their instruction and how they saw their classrooms change. And just like with our pilot group, the teachers from the expansion campuses had varied reactions to the program. We had a group of early adopters who couldn't wait to start, we had a group of teachers who were apprehensive but willing to give it a try, we had teachers with the "deer in the headlights" look, and we even had a teacher who had never used a cell phone before.

We handed out the MLDs to the teachers and spent time providing a functional overview. Once the overview was complete, we instructed the teachers to spend the next couple of weeks familiarizing themselves with the devices. We told them once school started there would be formal training sessions, at which time they would learn how to incorporate the MLDs into their lessons. With that, the teachers' introduction meeting was complete. Once again we had achieved our goals for the introduction, and the presentations from the pilot campus teachers gave the teachers from the expansion campuses valuable encouragement, reassurance, and practical advice. Most important, just like in our pilot year meeting, no teacher had run out screaming or objected to the concept of our program. All in all, we considered this meeting to be another huge success.

Teacher Training

For each campus we allotted two days of training for the teachers. In most cases, the principals participated in the training, reinforcing for their staffs their commitment to the program. Training was much easier in the second year because we had a year's worth of sample lessons from which to draw. Though we were moving device platforms, conceptually the lessons remained the same.

Initially, apprehension among the teachers was evident. However, as the training progressed and we were able to show the sample lessons and all of the support resources available, they seemed to be more comfortable with the idea. By the end of our two days of training, the majority of teachers appeared to be ready to start using the devices in their classrooms.

Parent Night Meetings

As we began planning for the parent night meetings, we faced two new challenges. First, we had bilingual campuses in our expansion pool and needed to provide both English and Spanish presentations, presenters, and documentation. Second, the expansion campuses were our highest free and reduced-price lunch campuses, and parents' attendance for school meetings was typically low.

Solving the bilingual problem was easy. We asked bilingual teachers at each campus to help with preparing the presentations and with documentation translation. The bilingual teachers were also asked to present at the meetings.

The parent night attendance issue was not as easy to solve. We decided that if we could get the children excited, they would have more influence on their parents' attending than anything we could send home. So we started right away talking with the students about the parent meeting and how if they wanted to get MLDs, their parents would need to attend. We also sent home many flyers and used our automated calling system, electronic campus news bulletin (eNews), and campus websites.

The agenda for the parent night was identical to what we used for the pilot group with two exceptions. We wanted to provide parents with a guide on appropriate use of these devices and the expectations we had for our students using them, so we created a responsible use guidelines document for MLDs. Additionally, we wanted to create video clips of our students and teachers using the devices in class throughout the year. These videos would be used in future discussions related to our strategic plan, so we created a student video permission form allowing KISD to video the MLD classes. The parent night agenda can be found at LennyJSchad.com.

Attendance for our parent nights amazed each of our expansion principals. Before every parent night meeting, each principal tried to prepare me for low attendance and spent time explaining this was not unusual and was something they struggled with all the time. They didn't want low attendance to reflect poorly on their campus or on enthusiasm for the project. To our surprise, *every one* of our parent night meetings was well attended. I think selling the students on the importance of the meeting was critical to our high turnout. The bilingual campus presentations went well, and I think the parents appreciated our efforts to have both English and Spanish versions of the presentation and translators there.

The Q&A portion of the meeting was very similar to our pilot year. Parents were concerned about lost or damaged devices and who would be responsible for replacement devices. Knowing the socioeconomic makeup of our campuses, I didn't want financial concerns to be a deterrent for the program, so we told parents that KISD would be responsible for lost or damaged devices. However, if it became apparent that a student was abusing this privilege, we would have to take a look at those situations case by case. For every one of our campuses, we once again had all the parents sign the consent form, and we felt that most parents understood our program and what it could do for their children.

Students Receive Devices

Handing out MLDs to the students was the best part of the rollout. To see the excited looks on their faces was magical. The first part of the day was spent providing the students with a basic overview of the devices. As you can imagine, this wasn't a long process. The last part of the day was spent teaching the students how to take care of their devices—how to store them, how to carry them, how to charge them, and the do's and don'ts. This was a great day everyone would long remember.

First MLD Lesson

The first MLD lesson was intentionally very basic, one that simply got the teacher and students used to the device and classroom management software. Depending on the teacher, the MLD support team would either model use of the device or lend support. The majority of support was simply getting the students acclimated to switching wireless networks and accessing Edmodo, our new classroom management application. Amazingly, it took only a couple days of hand-holding, and the classes were off and running.

Results

The results of our second year using MLDs in the classroom mimicked those seen in our pilot year. We had outstanding support from all of our principals, teachers, and parents. The teachers observed the same things occurring in their classrooms:

- immediate and sustained improved engagement
- increased time on task
- higher-level thinking skills
- creativity
- collaboration
- change in classroom dynamics

Here are some quotes from our teachers using MLDs in their classrooms:

> "The best thing I've seen is how excited the kids are about learning. They can't wait to use the MLDs for projects or to try new apps. We don't have to wait for our computer lab time or library time—they can find out what they need right away. They help each other out, challenge each other with questions, and make sure they all know what is going on in class."

> "The MLD is planting new seeds in the minds of all students, exposing them to dimensions they had no clue were available at their fingertips."

> "The MLDs have really made a huge difference in science. We are able to view videos and images and research science concepts. We use the camera to take pictures of different processes. The video feature is a great tool we use to capture a topic. Students love to explain and act out different experiments and terms."

"Having the MLDs in our classrooms and for use at home has greatly heightened my students' vocabularies, but more important they have become very interested in words and seek out better synonyms when they are writing. They are doing this without teacher reminders or prompting. We blog about books through Kidblog rather than writing book reports. We are using this site primarily as a book club and a forum for talking about literature that we are reading recreationally. As a result, students are seeking out other students to talk about books they are reading, discussing higher order features of books, and reflecting on themes."

Increased Availability of Applications

We saw a tremendous increase in the number of mobile-enabled applications available for education. Some of our most used mobile applications include:

Discovery Education. Allows teachers to assign lessons that are available online. Students access lesson objectives on their devices and proceed to complete the lessons by reading ebooks, watching video segments, completing virtual labs, and taking online quizzes.

Edmodo. Classroom management Web 2.0 tool used in MLD and non-MLD classrooms. Allows for class collaboration and communication, posting of assignments and grading, learning communities, and parental access.

Kidblog. Hosts student-created blogs, student-published posts, and classroom discussions. Includes a teacher administrative toolset for monitoring, reviewing, and deleting student-posted information.

PicSay. Allows students to label pictures taken with their mobile devices. For example, students can take pictures of objects and then label them with appropriate mathematical descriptions, such as cylinder, equilateral triangle, or quadrilateral.

QR Codes. Allows users to create a scanning code, used by the MLDs, that contains website addresses students will review to complete a homework assignment. This QR code can contain multiple web addresses and is an effective tool to ensure students are using the desired websites.

Quia. Allows for creation of online games and activities, creation of assessments, real-time tracking of student progress, and differentiated instruction.

Benchmark Scores

Once again, the real measurement for our second year was evaluating benchmark scores. Table 6.3 compares the average benchmark scores of the same group of students as fourth graders (2010, traditional instruction) and as fifth graders (2011, use of the MLDs).

TABLE 6.3 Comparison of average scores for the same group of students receiving traditional instruction in fourth grade (2010) and using the MLDs in fifth grade (2011).

Subject	Average scores Fourth Grade (2010) (traditional instruction)	Average scores Fifth Grade (2011) (instruction using MLDs)
Reading	91	93
Math	90	92
Science	NA*	90

Not applicable. There is no benchmark test for fourth grade science.

Table 6.4 compares the average scores of fifth graders at the 11 MLD campuses from 2010, when the students received traditional instruction, to 2011, when the students received MLD instruction.

TABLE 6.4 Comparison of average scores for fifth graders at MLD campuses receiving traditional instruction (2010) versus instruction using MLDs (2011).

Subject	Average scores Fifth Grade (2010) (traditional instruction)	Average Scores Fifth Grade (2011) (instruction using MLDs)
Reading	90	93
Math	91	92
Science	90	90

Just like in our pilot year, the results were impressive, particularly when you consider the pre-MLD scores were already in the 90th percentile. Statistically speaking, achieving improvement once students are in the upper percentiles is very difficult. Additionally, because these results were very similar to the pilot year, the MLD program begins to show more substantial proof of its direct correlation to the improvement.

Issues

Funding

Funding continued to be a concern. Although we did receive E-Rate funding for our MLD project, no changes were made to the E-Rate program to allow us to take advantage of any of that money in 2010–11. The program and any expansions had to be funded with district money.

Damage and Loss

Our damage and loss percentages were much higher than expected. We attributed the higher damage numbers to the protective cases. They weren't durable enough for fifth graders. We needed to spend a little more money and invest in a protective case that could withstand rougher treatment. From a loss perspective, our numbers were also higher than expected. While it was nice for parents not to be financially responsible for the devices, we needed to reconsider that strategy in preparation for the third year.

Discipline

From a discipline standpoint, we saw the need to formalize disciplinary actions and resulting consequences. We needed to document inappropriate behavior and give the appropriate consequence notice. On a number of occasions, students would lose the MLD privilege and not tell their parents why they lost it. The parents would call the school to ask why their child lost the privilege. If we had documented and sent home these actions, teachers, students, and parents would all be on the same page.

Balancing out our results with our issues, it was easy to conclude the MLD project was successful once again and should be continued. If at all possible, for Year Three we would look for expansion opportunities. However, those opportunities would have to be funded outside of KISD. The MLD program would receive no additional money for Year Three.

2011–12 School Year

As I mentioned in Chapter 1, KISD was one of 20 school districts awarded the U.S. Federal Communications Commission's (FCC's) "Learning on-the-Go" grant. This grant allowed E-Rate money to be used for mobile device data plans without location usage restrictions. We were able to take advantage of this grant for Year Three of the MLD project and expand to additional campuses.

Of the E-Rate money that we would receive, we calculated how much of our existing budget would be saved and used that cost savings to expand out to fifth grade classes at seven additional campuses for a total of 18 elementary campuses and 2,600 devices.

Keeping What Worked

For Year Three, we decided to continue with the Android operating system, which meant we could spend the summer tweaking existing lesson plans as well as creating new ones. This also gave us an opportunity to conduct some much-needed house cleaning in our knowledgebase and wiki. Other than that, nothing in regard to preparation changed for the third year.

We planned on using the same rollout implementation schedule, which was becoming standardized. A sample rollout schedule can be found at LennyJSchad.com. The plan of rolling out two MLD campuses per week still worked successfully. It provided schools with enough time and support such that by the end of the rollout week, the campus was fairly self-sufficient.

Addressing Discipline and Damage

We made several changes to address issues identified in Year Two.

To address discipline issues, we created two new forms. The first was the Inappropriate Use Notice. This form was used to document inappropriate behavior by a student with the MLD. The second form was Consequence Notice of Inappropriate MLD Use. This form was sent home with a student when disciplinary action was required. This was the process we used to keep the teacher, parent, and student all on the same page. Copies of both forms can be found at LennyJSchad.com.

To address our damage concern, we did two things. First we made sure to purchase a much more durable protective case. We ended up using an OtterBox case. We also met with the principals and asked them how we could get more financial responsibility from the parents. We all believed that because there was no financial liability, parental concern for how the students were taking care of the MLDs was not a top priority. The principals ended up classifying the MLDs just like textbooks and assigned the same replacement costs to MLDs that were lost or damaged. Parents, while not happy with the change in policy, were willing to adhere to the policy change. In fact, we didn't have a single student withdraw from the program as a result of the policy change. Both of the actions proved to be very good decisions as the number of broken devices in Year Three was significantly lower and was comparable to the first year.

Linking with High School App Developers

An exciting new wrinkle appeared in Year Three. It came to our attention in Year Two that a computer science teacher was teaching his students how to write applications for the Android market. This got me thinking of ways we could link the elementary MLD program into this teacher's instruction. As a result, after meeting and talking about options, we decided to try a pilot project in which the students in this high school computer science class would write applications for our fifth grade MLD program.

As part of the program, the high school students would go through the entire application development cycle, from requirements gathering, to prototyping, to final application creation. Talk about the circle of life! How amazing to think that our fifth grade students would be using applications on their MLDs that were written by KISD high school students. It was a great opportunity for all of our teachers and students.

The high school students were able to generate several MLD applications that were loaded onto the devices and used in fifth grade classrooms. One of the applications was a flash-card type game that was created to help students with math. Not only did the young developers experience firsthand the entire app life-cycle development process, they were able to see their applications being used by fellow students. Based on these results, we are planning to expand this program to our other high school computer science teachers.

Results

A requirement for the FCC "Learning on-the-Go" grant was that we prepare reports documenting progress and results of our MLD project. At the end of the year, we surveyed MLD teachers about their experiences using MLDs in the classroom. We also surveyed participating parents. The following data come from these surveys and were submitted in our preliminary report to the FCC.

Effect on Instruction

When asked what methods of instruction and strategies were affected by MLDs, teachers' responses included the following:

> *"As a bilingual teacher, I see how my students are improving their vocabulary and comprehension. They also have the opportunity to expand and build some prior knowledge by using Discovery Education, BrainPOP, etc."*

> *"Social learning and peer teaching/tutoring have been incredible. Students are eager to show what they have discovered and will help each other online at home when I am not available to them."*

> *"They are learning responsibility in an entirely new way—awesome!"*

> *"Learning how to research certain topics and peer interaction (teaching each other about MLDs and book club discussions on Edmodo) were both affected by MLDs."*

> *"Students are independently reading for information."*

> *"I find that I am able to assign various activities for students to work on within a certain time frame, which results in better time management for instruction and students. Most assignments are assigned via Edmodo with specific instructions for design and delivery."*

"[Benefits include] increased engagement on assignments, being able to use various sites as study guide resources for an upcoming test, connecting with fellow classmates about assignments, as well as connecting with the teacher after school hours about any misunderstanding of the homework."

"[MLDs allowed] web surfing activities and interactive activities through STEMScopes. Educational applications (Math Attack, etc.) improved student practice."

"We have used the MLDs to help teach story structure, branches of government, and the Bill of Rights activities using games on Quia. I have also used Edmodo to post review questions to my leveled groups about their reading passages. It has made spelling more interesting as they use the Ace Your Spelling Test app each week, as well as record the spelling of each word using the Voice Recorder app."

Off-Premises Use

The off-premises usage graph (Figure 6.1) shows the usage of our MLDs when students were away from the school building. Usage is indicated in kilobytes of information sent and received by the devices themselves. The data shows that in the first three months of students having the MLDs, at-home utilization increased each month. This is consistent with what we expected. As the students became more comfortable with the devices and tools, teachers were assigning more homework requiring that "at home" access. The slight dip in January, which is to be expected, reflected the students coming off winter break and needing time to get back into their routines. By February, the teachers and students were back in their routines and started leveraging the work done in the first semester to have the highest at home utilization.

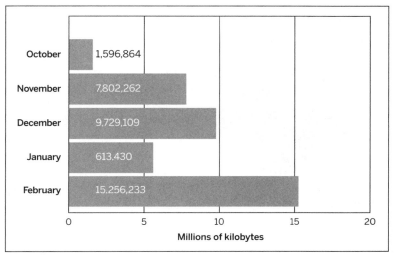

FIGURE 6.1   2011–12 Average MLD off-premises usage for all students

Implementation

The statistics in Figure 6.2 show the levels of implementation in the classroom and the effects they have had on teacher instruction and student learning. The data shows that roughly 75% of our classroom teachers used the MLDs from two to five days a week in their classrooms. Among the 25% of teachers who used the devices once a week or less in their classrooms, some taught noncore classes such as PE and music.

These statistics were encouraging because there were many other activities teachers were taking advantage of in the course of their daily instruction that did not require the use of MLDs. More important, it substantiated our claim to concerned parents that there was a time and place for MLDs in instruction and there was a time and place for other types of instructional delivery such as paper and pencil. Obviously the MLDs did not replace all traditional instructional methods.

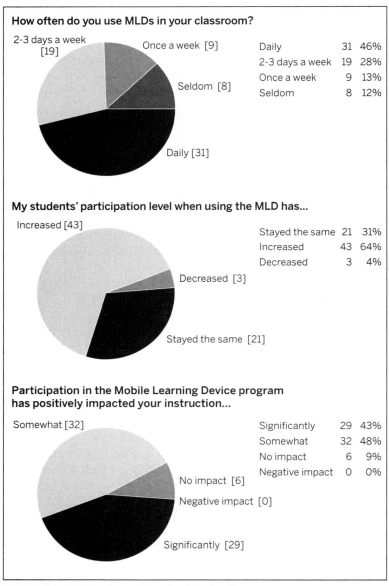

How often do you use MLDs in your classroom?

2-3 days a week [19]
Once a week [9]
Seldom [8]
Daily [31]

Daily	31	46%
2-3 days a week	19	28%
Once a week	9	13%
Seldom	8	12%

My students' participation level when using the MLD has...

Increased [43]
Decreased [3]
Stayed the same [21]

Stayed the same	21	31%
Increased	43	64%
Decreased	3	4%

Participation in the Mobile Learning Device program has positively impacted your instruction...

Somewhat [32]
No impact [6]
Negative impact [0]
Significantly [29]

Significantly	29	43%
Somewhat	32	48%
No impact	6	9%
Negative impact	0	0%

FIGURE 6.2   MLD implementation levels in the classroom

Test Scores

Figures 6.3 and 6.4 show the same groups of students' test scores for math and reading during the year they were using MLDs (2011) and the two years prior to having access. An analysis of the math scores shows the fifth grade class had a higher percentage increase in growth compared to the increased growth for the same cohort of students as fourth graders. While the percentage difference between the fourth and fifth grades was small, it was significant considering the "All Students" cohort was in the 90% range to begin with. The reading graph is more difficult to draw conclusions from. The fourth grade decline across all cohorts makes drawing any type of conclusion for the fifth grade year speculative at best. We can see there was marked improvement in the fifth grade year across all cohorts and considering there were not a lot of instructional or curricular changes, one could conclude the MLDs played a role in the increase.

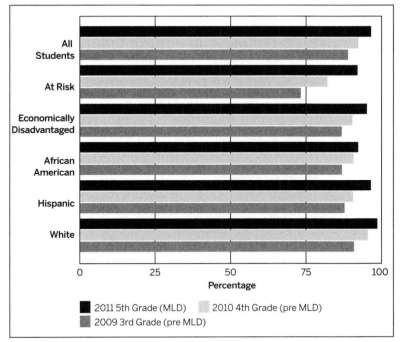

FIGURE 6.3 Comparison of same students' math scores before and during MLD use

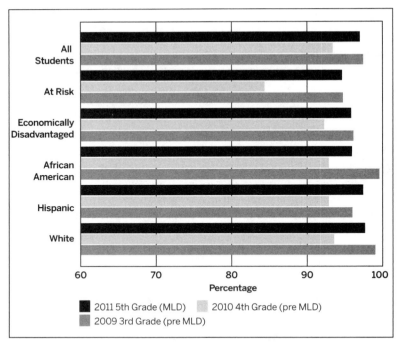

FIGURE 6.4 Comparison of same students' reading scores before and during MLD use

Figures 6.5, 6.6, and 6.7 show test scores for math, reading, and science of students in fifth grade who had MLDs (2011) and students from previous years (2010, 2009) who did not have MLDs. After analyzing these graphs we found it difficult to draw any conclusions regarding the MLD impact when comparing fifth grade classes. The results varied depending on the cohort and subject. What is interesting to note—when looking at individual campus comparisons the impact of MLDs was notable; for some campuses the impact was significant and for others that were already scoring high, the impact was minimal. When we combined all the schools together, the total impact was less identifiable.

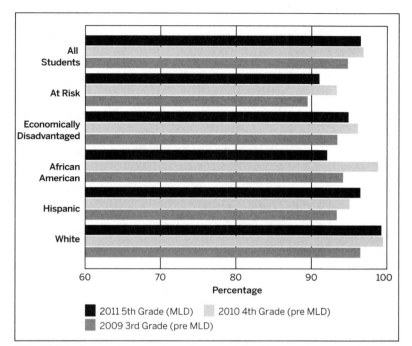

FIGURE 6.5   Comparison of fifth grade students' math scores before and during MLD use

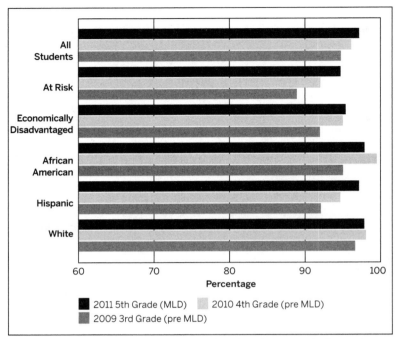

FIGURE 6.6 Comparison of fifth grade students' reading scores before and during MLD use

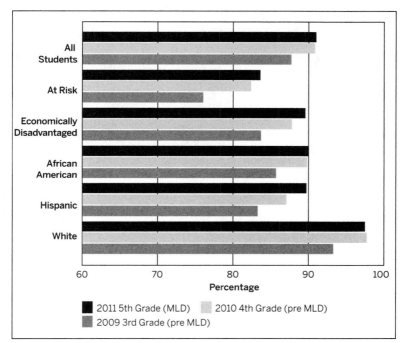

FIGURE 6.7   Comparison of fifth grade students' science scores before and during MLD use

Absenteeism

The absenteeism comparison chart (Figure 6.8) gives the statistics for absences. We found that absenteeism was the lowest in the year students were given the MLDs. This graph supports an assumption we had going into the MLD rollout. If students were engaged in the learning and had different modes or pathways to show comprehension, they would be more inclined to come to school, thus reducing the absenteeism rate.

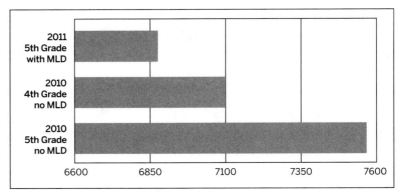

FIGURE 6.8 Absenteeism comparison

Behavioral Issues

There is a significant difference in the number of behavioral issues when comparing fifth grade students with MLDs and those without. (Figure 6.9) However, behavior problems showed a slight decline when the same students moved from fourth grade to fifth grade. Still, the fifth grade students the previous year (without MLDs) had almost twice the number of behavior incidents than students with MLDs. Therefore, a conclusion could be drawn that the use of MLDs helped with behavioral issues.

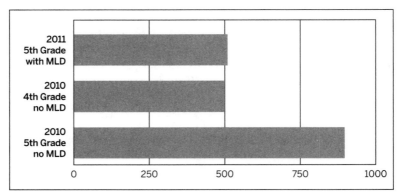

FIGURE 6.9 Behavior problems comparison

Parents

Parents have been overwhelmingly supportive of the mobile learning initiative at KISD. More than 680 parents completed a survey, and more than 80 percent made positive comments about the impact the devices and access at home have had on their child's education.

When parents were asked how often during a week's time their child experienced difficulty accessing the Internet at home on his or her MLD, they responded:

1 night/week:	14%
2 nights/week:	4%
3 nights/week:	7%
Never:	75%

Figure 6.10 shows further survey results; the following are some comments received from the open-ended portion of the parent survey.

Here is a sampling of comments from the participating parents:

> "The device made it where she was excited to finish homework, and it did not feel like doing homework."

> "In fact it has help my child on homework assignments that I'm not real sure about, and I really think the MLD is a very good device for students. It makes Miguel's education a better experience."

> "My son enjoys learning on the apps. They are really educational and make learning easier for him."

> "It's easier for my child to complete her assignments and homework. She sometimes plays her game apps, but mostly she is completing her Edmodo assignments. It's quick and much more comfortable than paperwork. So her MLD is a useful device for school."

> "This has been useful because he is able to finish his homework faster and always has access to different school topics that he can study in his spare time. Besides he never forgets his homework in the classroom desk."

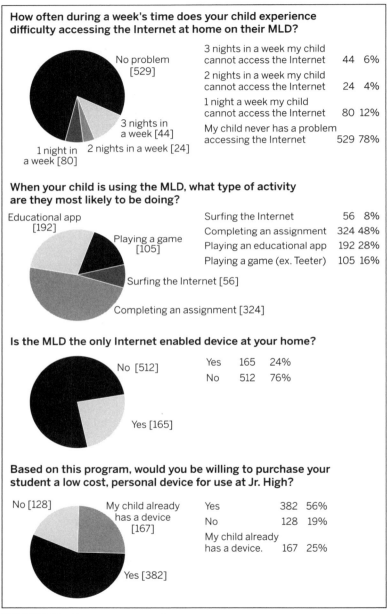

How often during a week's time does your child experience difficulty accessing the Internet at home on their MLD?

No problem [529]

3 nights in a week [44]

1 night in a week [80]   2 nights in a week [24]

3 nights in a week my child cannot access the Internet	44	6%
2 nights in a week my child cannot access the Internet	24	4%
1 night a week my child cannot access the Internet	80	12%
My child never has a problem accessing the Internet	529	78%

When your child is using the MLD, what type of activity are they most likely to be doing?

Educational app [192]

Playing a game [105]

Surfing the Internet [56]

Completing an assignment [324]

Surfing the Internet	56	8%
Completing an assignment	324	48%
Playing an educational app	192	28%
Playing a game (ex. Teeter)	105	16%

Is the MLD the only Internet enabled device at your home?

No [512]

Yes [165]

Yes	165	24%
No	512	76%

Based on this program, would you be willing to purchase your student a low cost, personal device for use at Jr. High?

No [128]

My child already has a device [167]

Yes [382]

Yes	382	56%
No	128	19%
My child already has a device.	167	25%

FIGURE 6.10   Parent survey results

Conclusion

As was the case in the previous two years, our Year Three results were very impressive. The devices proved to be tools that facilitated and enabled our teachers to change the ways they delivered classroom instruction. The devices had an immediate and sustainable impact on student engagement. And because of the improved student engagement, we saw our MLD students achieve more time on task, better test scores, and better attendance.

While funding continues to be the primary barrier to expanding our initiative, we are hopeful the FCC will recognize that mobile learning is not a luxury and is something our government should consider a priority from a funding perspective. Until that day comes, we will continue to explore creative ways to expand our program.

CHAPTER 7

Digital Citizenship Initiative

As we begin this chapter it is important to define "digital citizenship" and put it in context. Digital citizenship is a widely used term with varying definitions. Many people define digital citizenship simply as a set of guidelines on how to use technology appropriately. These guidelines are important, of course, and they were a component of this initiative; however, our definition of digital citizenship needed to extend far beyond that. Digital citizenship needed to encompass what it means for our students to be digital citizens—recognizing the realities of the digital world, understanding what students need to live and function successfully in the digital world, and being aware of the tools available to help them.

The traditional education model made digital citizenship the primary responsibility of IT Departments. Filtering systems were put in place to block students from accessing inappropriate content, monitoring systems were used to identify when inappropriate use occurred, and disciplinary systems were enacted when students broke the rules. Because of this "behind the scenes" prevention, digital citizenship instruction was never built into normal class time, and as a result we were not educating our students on what it meant to live responsibly in the digital world. With our three-year strategic plan, we were changing that traditional education model and our digital citizenship initiative was going to focus on educating the students of KISD not only to live in, but to participate responsibly and behave ethically in a 24/7 connected world.

Students were not the only group that would benefit from our digital citizenship initiative, as we learned from our early stakeholder group meetings. School board members, administrators, parents, and teachers all had need of a program that would help them better understand the digital world.

Parents told us that they did not really understand how much the digital world encompassed their children's lives, and this lack of understanding was creating a digital divide between them and their children. We saw that our digital citizenship initiative would need to extend beyond classroom instruction into the homes. The program would need to provide resources and guidelines to parents that would assist them with coming to terms with the digital world and more important, help them understand what parental guidance they could and should be providing to their children. We also recognized that introducing web-based tools and devices into the instructional process would foster questions and concerns from parents. If we did not make an effort to help parents understand the digital world and the significant role it played in their children's lives, getting them to accept this new instructional model would be more difficult. Because of these reasons, educating our parent community and reducing the divide became major goals of this initiative.

Just like the parents, our other stakeholders were experiencing their own digital divides and needed to have time to understand the digital world and the role it would play in the educational process. While we could offer professional development on tools and model instructional delivery, if we did not spend time with them bridging the divide, the cultural change would never become institutionalized. Our digital citizenship initiative would need to start at the grass-roots level and focus on the same basics and fundamentals needed by parents.

As we began to formalize the components of our digital citizenship initiative, the goals and objectives became very clear. Through the digital citizenship initiative, we wanted to achieve a basic level of understanding from our stakeholders regarding the strategic plan and what we were trying to achieve. Once we had understanding from our stakeholders, we could then leverage the program to obtain acceptance. Understanding and acceptance are two very important elements in any strategic plan; without them your plan is in jeopardy.

Obtaining understanding and acceptance were not going to be quick processes and we didn't want to rush the program or make our stakeholders feel like it was being pushed down their throats. Because this process was so critical to the overall success of our three-year plan, we decided to dedicate Year One of our digital citizenship program to introducing fundamental concepts and fostering a baseline level of understanding of what we were doing, why we were doing it, and how we were going to do it. Year Two would leverage the basic understanding accomplished in Year One and begin focusing on moving our stakeholders to acceptance of our strategic goal and direction. If we were successful in achieving fundamental acceptance of our plan, the focus in Year Three and beyond would be a continued reduction of the digital divide between stakeholders and students and the ongoing education and alignment of our stakeholders with district strategies regarding digital transformation.

Our initiative would include the following focus areas, which together formed the digital citizen framework from which we would work:

> **Internet Safety.** This includes practices and precautions Internet users should observe to ensure their personal information and computer remain safe.

> **Privacy and Security.** This includes practices Internet users should consider when using sites requiring any personal information or settings that make information public.

> **Appropriate Communication.** This includes communication practices that should be considered when using social networking sites.

> **Digital Footprints.** This includes concepts surrounding the data trail left by any user of the Internet through various types of interactions in a digital environment.

Information Literacy. This includes defining the necessary set of skills needed to find, retrieve, analyze, and use information via the Internet.

Content Management and Copyright. This includes practices that should be incorporated when using content or copyrighted materials from the Internet.

2009–10 School Year

Changing District Guidelines

For Year One, we knew what our focus areas would be; we just needed the opportunity to start the digital citizenship conversations. As preparations began for the upcoming school year, KISD conducted its annual review of district guidelines. One of the documents reviewed was the Acceptable Use Guidelines (AUG). There were already going to be some modifications to the existing AUG to accommodate our Web 2.0 integration initiative; however, I also wanted to leverage this document as a starting point for digital citizenship conversations. During the review process I recommended we change the name from Acceptable Use Guidelines to Responsible Use Guidelines (RUG). Changing the name might seem like a small thing, but it caused KISD staff members to begin asking "Why?" Our answer to this question was simple: as a district we didn't want just *acceptable* use from our staff and students; we wanted *responsible* use from those accessing our software and using our tools. The internal process for changing the title allowed us to discuss why we were changing it with a small group of stakeholders.

The process review consisted of multiple meetings that provided me with valuable insights into how big a role our digital citizenship framework would play in the overall success of our strategic plan. We met with administrators, teachers, and parents to talk about the differences between acceptable and responsible use. These conversations allowed us to begin defining responsible use and outlining those areas of focus in our digital citizenship framework. They also became our entry point, with a small subset of stakeholders to introduce digital citizenship. During the meetings I saw firsthand how important digital citizenship and the focus areas were going to be in the overall success of our strategic initiative. If we had simply made the Web 2.0–specific changes to the AUG, we would have encountered pushback from our stakeholders because the changes would have been centered on tools rather than responsible use and appropriate behavior. But because we started by discussing the name change and differences between acceptable and responsible use, this allowed us to talk about the digital citizenship framework first. There were no objections from the committee members in our conversations regarding the digital citizenship framework. Everyone agreed the focus areas clearly defined what we meant by the term *responsible,* and it was easy for them to understand and accept why a change in the name was important.

With our stakeholder review committee in agreement with the name change, we then changed the focus to content changes in the RUG. We already had a foundation, the digital citizenship framework, from which to make the content changes. The first-year changes to the RUG were very basic and in two specific areas. First, we allowed access to social networking sites at the district's and teachers' discretion. Even though the stakeholders understood the digital citizenship framework, the term *social networking* still had an immediate negative connotation, especially for the parents. However, if we (KISD and the stakeholders) were serious about preparing children to live responsibly in a digital world, the children needed to have access to the same tools inside the classroom as they have access to outside the classroom. This concept took time and lots of conversations to convey; however, the review committee eventually came to understand the need for social networking inside the classroom.

The key to getting consensus from this group was reassuring them that any social networking site would have to be vetted by the Curriculum Department to ensure curricular alignment and by the Technology Department to ensure the necessary safety elements were in place, such as controlled access, monitoring, and filtering. This was the same process that we put in place for any Web 2.0 tool introduced into the KISD environment.

The second change in our existing policy was to allow use of mobile devices in the classroom. With the MLD pilot kicking off, we needed to make sure this change was in place before we began. This change wasn't as big an issue for our stakeholders as the social networking change. The biggest concern for the stakeholders was how we could limit the allowance to the campus conducting the MLD pilot program. Once again we grounded the discussion in the digital citizenship framework and showed how the devices could be leveraged in our focus areas. The group agreed to modify our device policy to say mobile devices could be used in the classroom at the teacher's discretion.

The final step in the RUG process was presenting the name and content changes to the school board. The review process prepared me very well for the types of questions and concerns I could expect from the school board. I used the same process when presenting this topic to the board. I focused first on the name change and introducing our digital citizenship framework and then moved to how the content changes enabled us to begin educating our students on the various focus areas. We also had representation at the meeting from the campus and parent community. This helped the school board accept our recommendations, especially those concerning social networking. This turned out to be one of the most productive presentations I had ever given to the school board. I walked away from the meeting feeling like they really understood what we were trying to accomplish and would support our tactics for change. If we had any hope of accomplishing the goals of the strategic plan we needed to have the support of our school board, administrators, teachers, and parents—not just at the beginning but also when we encountered the inevitable bumps in the road. All too often if there is no support, the immediate response to problems is to take the path of least resistance and abandon the initiative. But with support from all stakeholders, we could adjust, re-evaluate, and stay the course.

Digital Citizenship Content

With the responsible use guidelines now approved, we turned our focus to creating digital citizenship content for the classrooms. With most of our Instructional Technology Team time dedicated to Web 2.0 and MLDs, I didn't want to spend time recreating content from scratch if it was already out there. The team began researching digital citizenship content that was published specifically for the K–12 space. We found a number of age-appropriate publications that provided free content for teachers, parents, and students.

The best sources of digital citizenship content were the Federal Trade Commission (FTC) and Common Sense Media. Both of these organizations provide school systems with free materials for students and parents. We distributed the FTC's booklet *Heads Up!*, part of a free resource toolkit called *Net Cetera*, to every student at the beginning of school. *Net Cetera* was also a great resource for the parents as we introduced Web 2.0 tools and MLDs. The booklet can be found online (www.onguardonline.gov/features/feature-0004-featured-net-cetera-toolkit) or can be bulk ordered (http://bulkorder.ftc.gov). For teachers we decided to focus on guidelines they could use during their instructional periods. Not wishing to overload everyone in our first year, we were cognizant of how much and how often we handed out materials.

With sources for digital citizenship content identified, the Instructional Technology Team wanted to immediately begin creating lessons and modeling strategies. However, they had to put that on hold in order to get ready to meet with larger groups of administrators, teachers, and parents to further broadcast our message. These stakeholder groups would want more than lesson plans and modeling strategies to convince them. The first step was to modify documents we used in the school board meeting for specific stakeholder groups. This actually didn't take much time as we had put so much thought and effort into the original material. This repurposing also gave the Instructional Technology Team an opportunity to solidify their approach and communication strategy for each stakeholder group.

Once we were satisfied that we were ready to introduce our digital citizenship framework, the team then began working on lesson plans and modeling strategies, using the digital citizenship framework and focus areas do drive content. The lesson plans and strategies also needed to be closely linked to the tools in our Web 2.0 toolboxes .

As we reflected on the focus areas, we realized that each focus area had an applicable age range. It wouldn't be possible to create a one-stop digital citizenship framework for all age groups. Therefore, when creating the lesson plans and modeling strategies, we needed to be mindful of the age group and applicable elements of the framework. This proved to be fairly easy for our older students, but more of a challenge for younger students. We knew that even our kindergarten students needed some introduction into digital citizenship, so it was very important to identify the Web 2.0 tools our younger students would be using and apply the framework focus areas specifically for each age group.

The team had a tendency to try to do too much too fast so I had to remind them that our goal for Year One was to gain an understanding of digital citizenship among our stakeholder communities. We needed to slow down and make sure the pace of information output allowed the stakeholders time to absorb the information and formulate any questions or concerns. There was a wealth of digital citizenship information out there, but disseminating it too fast would compromise the understanding process.

Face-to-Face Meetings

To introduce the digital citizenship framework, we needed as many face-to-face meetings with our stakeholders as possible. For this critical topic, it wasn't enough to send out a single flyer or meet only once with teachers or parent groups. We needed to have multiple conversations with the same groups to achieve a solid foundation of understanding for our framework. The Instructional Technology director and I spent a lot of time attending meetings on all campuses to get out our message. We weren't alone. Everyone in the

Instructional Technology Team looked for opportunities to discuss the topic as well, which is why it was so important to spend the time formalizing our communication strategies around our presentations. Consistency of our messaging was critical particularly in the introductory phase of this initiative.

The following sections describe some of the meetings where we discussed digital citizenship.

Meetings with Principals

We knew if we were to achieve any kind of success with our strategic plan and our Year One goals, it would take the understanding, acceptance, commitment, and fidelity of our campus principals. This is the leadership level that would ensure the expectations of our teachers would be monitored and managed. These are also the individuals who have the most influence over their parent communities. We took the presentation from the school board meeting and met with each principal. Most of the principals were aware of the three-year plan but did not have a thorough understanding of the initiatives and how we wanted the campuses to implement them. I wanted to make sure the pace at which we were implementing the initiatives was at a level the principals felt comfortable with. I wanted to make sure they understood the digital citizenship framework and the role it played supporting the other two initiatives. Most important, I wanted them to understand the support mechanisms that were in place for them to use during the implementation. If the principals were comfortable with the plan and the implementation pacing and felt a strong sense of support from the central office, they would take ownership and get the buy-in from their teachers. The initial presentations were very well received by this level of leadership. I felt each principal understood what was expected in Year One and their role in helping to achieve the goals. While I don't think we had full commitment from every principal (a few were initially skeptical), overall our initial meetings were productive. It was important that throughout the year my department touched base with the principals as often as possible. It was this personal interaction that ensured the sense of commitment was sustained throughout the implementation.

Campus Staff Meetings

These were meetings held by the campus principals with their staff members—perfect gatherings for our introductory presentation. It was important to have the principal lead the presentation because it showed their staff the principal's commitment to the digital citizenship framework and three year strategic plan. It was an opportunity for the teachers to understand the expectations for the first year and what they could expect in the way of changes. Because this was a very large group meeting, it did not afford the opportunity for a lot of questions; however, achieving a high level of understanding from just one meeting was not our goal or even realistic. Rather, our objectives in this meeting were for the staff to see the commitment of their principal, what was expected in Year One, and, most important, a high-level view of what was going to change. Just like the principals, we wanted the teachers to walk away from the meeting understanding that this was a district commitment with plenty of support from the central office.

This was the only time my team met with the entire campus staff. However, my team was on every campus numerous times a week—meeting with PLC groups, department heads, and individual teachers, conducting training sessions using sample lessons plans, modeling instruction in the classrooms, and observing classroom instruction.

Leadership Katy

In the Leadership Katy program, members of our community are selected to spend a year learning about the operations of a school district. The group meets once a month, and each department in the district has an opportunity to discuss its role in the district. The intent is to create a group of knowledgeable community members who can speak to various issues, become champions for the district, and be positive voices in the community. The Technology Department used its month to introduce responsible use and our digital citizenship framework. It was critical to get the group members to support our strategic plan because they were viewed as community leaders. We used the format and sequencing of our presentation that had worked so well with other groups. We introduced the concept of responsible use and talked about our framework to achieve it, building a foundation for the group members to understand our program. We concluded our presentation with a high-level overview of our three-year strategic plan. I believe that if we had led with the strategic plan, we would have encountered more concerns about it. After this meeting we had a group of community members who could speak knowledgeably about our direction.

PTA/PTO Meetings

I held an initial meeting with the presidents of our Parent-Teacher Association (PTA) and Parent-Teacher Organizations (PTOs) from all campuses, using the same presentation with them that I used with Leadership Katy. My goal for this initial meeting was simply to walk through our presentation and answer some of their questions. I knew that this group of involved parents would require multiple conversations as we needed to allow them plenty of time to absorb the information. I talked with this group about our desire to have multiple meetings with their campus groups and how important it was for their campus organizations to fully understand KISD's plans for the next three years. These are powerful groups of parents and ones you want on your side. While the presidents had many questions, they were more than willing to have members of my team come talk about our presentation with their campus teams. In the first year we had multiple meetings with this group of parents, and they proved to be great resources as we moved along with the first year implementation.

Reflecting back on the initial meeting, I realized I should have had separate meetings with the presidents from each level (i.e., elementary presidents, junior high presidents, and high school presidents). The concerns at each level were different enough that trying to address them all in one meeting was a challenge. I didn't sense we had achieved the level of understanding that I wanted. However, in the subsequent campus meetings, we were able to achieve very high levels of understanding and support.

Open Houses

We took advantage of open houses because they brought out parents who typically don't go to a lot of school meetings. These parents will attend start-of-school open houses to meet the teacher(s) and principal, and in some cases that will be the last campus meeting they attend all year. So open houses were an important opportunity to speak directly to a hard-to-reach group of parents. After our presentation at the open house, an interesting thing occurred. Many of our principals found that any time they had a technology update on a campus meeting agenda, it was one of the most well-attended meetings that year. This was an indication to my team that this subset of parents was interested. It was our hope that their interest would turn into understanding.

Superintendent's Leadership Meetings

Once a month, typically the day after the school board meeting, the superintendent will bring in leadership from around the district and spend the morning talking about various topics. Attendees are usually director-level and above, as well as all campus principals. Each of the superintendent's cabinet members has an opportunity to present to this group. We presented multiple times to this group of leaders throughout the first year, first giving them our introductory presentation and then providing updates on our strategic plan. We also received a lot of very good feedback. Often the feedback was from outsiders, leaders from various departments with different points of view who would voice concerns or make helpful suggestions about solutions that we had not considered.

I have mentioned this before but it is worth repeating—consistency of messaging is one of the most important elements in the overall success of a strategic plan. The district leaders at this meeting needed to have a thorough understanding of our three-year strategic plan and our expectations for the year. It was also important that they understood the message we were communicating to our teachers and parents. Digital citizenship was applicable to and the responsibility of every employee in KISD, so it was important that everyone was receiving the same message.

Once this meeting concluded, the principals (grouped by school level) would meet together in the afternoon. My team leveraged these meetings to introduce topics specifically focused on the particular principal group, as well as to receive feedback from them. These meetings were some of the most productive times we spent with principals. They allowed my department to address unique issues facing a particular age group of students. More important they provided an opportunity for the principals to share and collaborate among their peers on issues or solutions that were occurring on their campuses.

Employee Roundtable

The Employee Roundtable comprised one representative teacher from each of our campuses; they brought issues and concerns from their campuses to the cabinet. The cabinet also had the opportunity to present to this group. Our presentations to this group focused on updates regarding the various initiatives, as well as updates regarding issues or concerns brought up in previous group meetings. The greatest value of these meetings for us was hearing from our teacher community, especially their perceptions of the initiatives and where they were struggling with the implementation process.

The majority of questions for us the first year focused on the Web 2.0 tools and the fact that teachers wanted more training opportunities. We didn't get a lot of questions regarding out digital citizenship framework and focus areas. When we inquired about the framework and how it was being used in the classrooms, the feedback was positive. The degree of implementation of the framework varied among the campuses and seemed to be directly linked to how many of the campus teachers were embracing the Web 2.0 tools. The exception was our MLD campus. Under the exceptional leadership of the campus principal, the framework was being integrated heavily with the fifth grade team as well as all the other grade levels.

These meetings were also an opportunity to gauge how much the principals were driving the goals of our strategic plan. Teachers would often comment about the progress their school was making with a particular initiative compared to other schools. By listening to the comments and their tone, we got a good sense if the principal was truly leading the effort and being a champion or was taking a back seat and relying on the central office to drive the plan. We used the issues brought to this meeting in our conversations with principals to see if they were in touch with the climate of their teachers and to point out areas they might want to focus on with a little more effort.

Additionally, these meetings allowed the teachers to learn from each other. Teachers found common concerns and shared how their particular campuses were addressing the issues. It was very clear in these meetings how much campus cultures varied within our district.

Student Roundtable

The Student Roundtable was made up of representatives from each of our high schools. The roundtable met a few times throughout the course of a school year. These students showed us just how well our initiatives were really working and we utilized our time with them to gather information on a number of fronts.

First, we inquired about how much the Web 2.0 tools were being used in their daily instruction. Their responses indicated that adoption of the tools varied with every campus and even within each content area. This again reflected how much the campus leadership was pushing the strategic plan and our first year goals. When asked if they liked using the tools, the students' responses mirrored what we learned in an initial stakeholder meeting with students. They liked using the tools because they were familiar with them, they already used these tools outside the classroom in their personal lives to learn, and, most important, the tools were a change from the daily instructional grind.

Second, we talked to the students about the digital citizenship framework and the relevance of focus areas to their age group. We were able to see how the framework focus areas were being discussed in our high schools. The students' feedback was positive, and our meetings generated great discussions among the students. This group recognized the need to discuss digital citizenship issues in school because their only source of information was their peers, who were basically in the same boat. The students told us about trying to have conversations with their parents about some of these topics and how "out of touch" they were. This reinforced to us the need to provide parents with every opportunity and resource in the digital citizenship program so that they could begin to communicate with their children about responsible use.

We also used these meetings to talk with the students about how they were using social networking, how they were using their personal devices, and if they saw educational relevance of these tools in the classroom. Through our discussions regarding the tools they use outside the classroom and what they would like to see change on their campuses we (KISD) were even more committed to the strategic plan. The ways the students used the tools outside the classroom were exactly what we were hoping to bring into the schools through our initiatives. In fact, most of the students' wish lists of what could change were part of what we hoped would be accomplished through our strategic plan. When asked about concerns with the strategic plan and direction, students' most consistent response was equity. They recognized that not every student had a device or Internet access at home and were concerned about this issue.

I always enjoy talking to students; they don't pull any punches, and they tell it like it is. It is a shame that so many of the initiatives school districts embark on leave out this very important group of stakeholders. It is my belief that including this group and listening carefully to students' feedback will provide a stronger foundation for the implementation of any initiative.

Technology Showcases

Various campuses held technology showcase nights for parents throughout the year. These are traditionally well attended because they give parents the opportunity to see their children's work. We took advantage of these events to introduce our digital citizenship framework as well as Web 2.0 tools to more members of the parent community.

The first showcase of the year started with our introductory digital citizenship framework presentation to the group. We then divided the attendees into groups and had three breakout sessions they would rotate through. One session focused on the digital citizenship framework, another session focused on our Web 2.0 toolbox and demonstrations of some of the tools, and the third session covered peripheral equipment used on campus, such as interactive whiteboards, science probes, and laptop carts. If the showcase night was at an elementary school or junior high, we concluded the evening by inviting high school students to participate in a panel discussion on how they used technology. The students shared the role technology played in their lives and how they used their personal devices. We wanted to show the parents of our younger students that these personal devices were not toys, but significant components of how these students lived. We also gave parents an opportunity to ask the students questions. In every case, the panel discussion ran long because parents had so many questions.

Subsequent showcase events included less time for the group meeting and jumped right into the breakout sessions. The breakout session topics stayed the same, but as the year progressed, we were able to incorporate work done by the students. This was important because parents began to see the practical applications of these tools in the education of their children. Additionally, it gave the parents an opportunity to see how easy it was for their children to embrace these tools and demonstrate true understanding. Some parents were amazed at their children's creativity because they had no idea of their abilities to use technology.

These showcases were a highly effective way to develop acceptance and support for our three-year plan and associated initiatives. I highly recommend incorporating technology showcases into any rollout strategy.

First-Year Reflections

To close out the first year of the digital citizenship initiative, I created a short video for our high school and junior high students about social networking. The video included information about various social networking sites, housekeeping tasks they should perform on a regular basis, and the realities of posting content—how what you post today could come back to hurt you in the future. I also gave them some thoughts about managing friends and what to consider when accepting friends. The intent was to provide students with some thinking points about social networking as they headed out for summer break.

I was surprised by how much positive feedback I received from teachers and parents about the video. Obviously, it was nice to receive thanks for providing information that they thought was valuable. But the feedback was also eye opening, because all parents and teachers I talked with regarding the video said they learned something new; in some cases, the parents had no idea what social networking was or what risks it carried. So educating the parents was still going to be every bit as important as educating our students when it came to going forward with the digital citizenship initiative. We had a huge opportunity as an educational system to provide tremendous value to our community with this project.

As I reflected on the results of the first year of digital citizenship, I knew we had accomplished our objective of introducing the digital citizenship framework and strategic plan to our stakeholders. We had taken every opportunity to engage in conversations about the initiative with our school board, superintendent, administration, principals, teachers, parents, and students.

However, understanding of the digital citizenship initiative varied among our stakeholder groups. We achieved true understanding and support from our school board, most of our principals, the early adopters of the Web 2.0 toolboxes, the MLD pilot campus, and students. With the parents and our non-early adopter teachers, I believe we achieved only a philosophical understanding, meaning that they understood *why* we needed to change, but had difficulty understanding the tactical methods for *how* we were going to accomplish this fundamental change to the traditional education model. I believed for this group of stakeholders absorbing all this new information was like standing in front of a fire hydrant, trying to take a drink of water.

My clue that this was happening was paradoxically the lack of pushback from our parent community in the first year. There were two ways to look at this. Optimistically, we had done such a good job achieving understanding with all stakeholders, they had moved into the acceptance stage and were fully onboard. We were ahead of schedule. Realistically, we were facing a large group of teachers who weren't early adopters and parents whose children weren't yet in classes that used Web 2.0 tools. They simply didn't have a level of understanding or enough information to generate pushback—yet. While I like to be the eternal optimist, I do have to be realistic. I decided our second scenario was far more likely, and we needed to take this into consideration as we began planning for Year Two.

While we felt a great sense of accomplishment, I knew that unless we could get these parents, teachers, and principals to understand how the changes worked, we would not be successful in accomplishing the goals of the strategic plan.

2010–11 School Year

Our primary objective for Year Two of the initiative was moving all stakeholders closer to acceptance of our digital citizenship framework and strategic plan. For this purpose, we divided stakeholders into two groups. For stakeholders who had only a philosophical understanding of the "why," our goal was to move them toward authentic understanding of the "how." For the stakeholders who had achieved authentic understanding, our goal was to move them to acceptance.

We also identified another, increasingly urgent digital citizenship issue that needed to be addressed in our district as well—cyberbullying. Cyberbullying was becoming a topic of concern for every school system in the country. It seemed like not a month would pass without some type of cyberbullying situation making national, state, or local news. The objective for the Instructional Technology Team would be to identify the focus areas in our framework related to cyberbullying and provide our campuses with resources and lessons to better educate our students on this topic.

With our objectives for Year Two clearly defined, we spent the summer before our second year working in the following areas:

Lesson plans. The team began working with the Curriculum Department, integrating digital citizenship concepts and resources into our Web 2.0 and MLD lesson plans. We were able to leverage the experience of the early adopters from Year One to greatly expand the breadth and depth of lesson plans we could make available in our curriculum management system.

Knowledgebase. The Instructional Technology Team expanded the knowledgebase, adding content generated from Year One. We added many new examples of how teachers could integrate Web 2.0 tools and our digital citizenship framework into specific content instruction.

Portals. The team implemented digital citizenship sections within our elementary and secondary portals, similar to the Web 2.0 sections. We wanted to create a space where students and parents could get more information related to digital citizenship. It was important to give parents a resource they could access from anywhere to research and gather specifics about particular issues they were struggling with. We felt that both students and parents would be comfortable with this type of self-service resource.

Collaboration. One of the things I witnessed in the face-to-face meetings from Year One was the power of collaboration. When we gave people the opportunity to discuss issues or concerns in a group setting, the group provided invaluable insights, experiences, and solutions. We needed to leverage this concept in ways that could extend beyond face-to-face meetings. One of the ways we did this was by creating two digital citizenship wikis, one for our teachers and one for the parents. These would be spaces where the Instructional Technology Team could post links specific to teachers or parents with resources, articles, and guidelines, as well as post questions. In return it was a space for these groups to collaborate with each other.

Cyberbullying and social networking etiquette. One of the most frequent ways students were being bullied was via social networking sites. So we used our framework focus areas to specifically address cyberbullying and social networking etiquette. The Instructional Technology Team found a number of useful resources dedicated to addressing these issues, and we were able to incorporate them into the classroom curriculum.

Presentations. We planned to leverage the same face-to-face meetings from Year One in order to further our conversations about the initiative in Year Two. The challenge was to create a presentation that would have an impact on both groups of stakeholders. We added examples of student work, achievement data, and teacher comments from Year One to add credibility to and validate our three-year plan. Having hard data is an advantage when speaking to any group. It was especially beneficial to us when dealing with parents.

Focus on Librarians

There was one group of district employees with whom we didn't spend much time in Year One—librarians. In retrospect, I realized librarians should have been one of our key stakeholder focus groups. Librarians are teachers with a direct link to digital citizenship and how to use the Internet for research. With so much research being done via the Internet, we needed librarians to fully embrace our digital citizenship framework and incorporate proper methodologies into their lessons. Plus, this is the group of teachers who would help students understand that just because it says so in Wikipedia, doesn't make it a fact! As we began introducing the framework and related focus areas to our librarians, we experienced the same reactions as for our Web 2.0 and MLD rollouts. Some librarians immediately embraced the framework and jumped right into incorporating it. Others were apprehensive and needed multiple sessions before they bought into the approach. Still another group thought we were way off base and simply opposed it. Just like with our other initiatives, we knew everyone needed time to come to terms with what we were doing, so for Year Two we focused on the librarians who were the most enthusiastic and had embraced the digital citizenship framework. As you might have noticed, the impact of pacing on adoption is a reoccurring theme in this book. We never wanted any of our stakeholders to feel like the strategic plan and associated initiatives were being pushed down their throats, particularly in the early years of implementation. Adoption needed to occur organically, and we needed to give our stakeholders time to understand our goals.

Stakeholder Pushback

It was in the latter part of our first semester in Year Two that we saw an awakening from our parent community in regard to Web 2.0 tools and digital citizenship. When I say the parent community woke up, I mean they became vocal. We received much more pushback than in Year One. With many more teachers embracing the Web 2.0 tools and more conversations occurring in the classrooms related to our digital citizenship framework, increasing numbers of parents were starting see this change of instruction in multiple ways. They were seeing their children's homework look completely different when teachers used Web 2.0 tools. Their children were talking to them more about topics related to digital citizenship. This increase of awareness in the parent community brought forward concerns about some of the Web 2.0 tools teachers were using and some digital citizenship issues. These concerns were brought not just to our attention—they were brought to the attention of every PTA/PTO organization, presented in open forums at our school board meetings, and published in local blogs and websites.

This was the first real test of our strategic plan. Did we do enough in the area of understanding and did we do enough to have our stakeholders maintain their support, and withstand this first real pushback? While most issues brought to our attention were resolved in a way that left both sides comfortable (see Chapter 5), some parents were unwilling to compromise on some issues. In those cases, we had to agree to disagree.

Second-Year Reflections

Year Two proved to be the most challenging yet most rewarding of our three-year strategic plan. Just like in the first year, the face-to-face meetings moved the needle for both of our stakeholder areas of focus: philosophical to real understanding and real understanding to acceptance. I believe that adding student work, achievement data, and teacher comments to our presentations gave the necessary levels of credibility to move our stakeholders in the right direction.

Proof that we not only had achieved understanding regarding what we were trying to accomplish with our goal and initiatives, but we had achieved acceptance from a large portion of stakeholders came from their reaction to the pushback. This type of resistance could have derailed the entire strategic plan and would have been the perfect jumping-off point for any one of our stakeholder groups. But while some of the oppositional parents sought to gain public support for their specific issues, they found little support among the stakeholder groups. Through each one of the concerns, not once did the school board, superintendent, principals, or teachers involved with the concern question or waver regarding our strategic goal and associated initiatives.

Cyberbullying became a much more visible element of our digital citizenship framework. My team was able to provide valuable resources to all our campuses. Conversations about cyberbullying were occurring throughout the schools, particularly at the secondary level. In our face-to-face meetings with parents, it was consistently a topic of conversation. Parents were very involved in the education process related to this topic, and the involvement increased with each news story in the media.

Our librarians proved to be a valuable addition to the implementation process. Their ability to incorporate so many of the digital citizenship framework focus areas into their instruction had an immediate beneficial impact on our students and teachers. Their involvement was not limited to the framework; they also began incorporating Web 2.0 tools into their instruction.

2011–12 School Year

As we began planning for the third year, we evaluated the actions taken in the prior two years to identify any gaps we felt existed in our implementation. In our evaluation process, we determined that while we had increased the number of stakeholders accepting the strategic plan, we couldn't declare victory and ignore those who hadn't moved from understanding to acceptance. We discovered something interesting in our evaluation of progress—a larger percentage of our teaching force had embraced the digital citizenship framework compared to Web 2.0 tool adoption. As a result, we wanted to leverage the momentum behind our digital citizenship framework to reduce the lag that existed with the Web 2.0 tools. This was going to be much more difficult, given the reduction of our Instructional Technology Team from 26 members to four (as discussed in Chapter 5).

We wanted once again to leverage face-to-face meetings, this year with the objective of showing tighter integration between our digital citizenship framework and Web 2.0 tools. We now had two years' worth of content in our curriculum management system, and our knowledgebase had a wealth of resources our teachers could use in their classrooms. It was also time to focus on the campus leadership to ensure they were driving adoption for those teachers who had yet to embrace the initiatives. At this point in the implementation, principals needed to decide what kind of targeted interventions they would implement for the teachers who were not embracing the tools and changing their instructional delivery, up to and including determining KISD was probably not the school district for these teachers.

For Year Three, we added a new topic to our digital citizenship presentations—BYOD. Beginning in Year Three, BYOD became available at all KISD campuses. We knew there would be some concerns and questions related to this program, and we wanted to include this topic in our presentations. This was such a natural progression in our digital citizenship framework, incorporating BYOD resources and content was not difficult. In fact, we were expecting much more resistance from the parents in our face-to-face meetings than we ever received. This proved to us that the time and energy we had spent with the parents on the framework in the two years leading up to BYOD established a solid foundation. More details about our BYOD rollout will be discussed in Chapter 8.

In Year Three, an organizational change for our district occurred right before the start of school. Now, all the librarians would not only report to their principal, but would also report to the Instructional Technology director. I was excited—I had been working on this change for two years. We had seen firsthand from Year Two that librarians were an untapped resource; each one would have an important role at every campus as we moved into the digital world.

The first thing we did was change the job title and descriptions. Similar to the change from the AUG to the RUG, this action started conversations with group about what KISD envisioned as its role in the digital age. The new title was Library Media Specialist. Because we had started working with this group in the prior year on digital citizenship, the process of getting buy-in for this change was not as hard as you might think. Most important, by changing the title and job description, this group of teachers had a very clear description of what we expected from them.

Our third year was similar to the first year in that there was minimal parental pushback, once again validating our premise that we had committed stakeholders who had accepted and were supportive of our strategic plan. The most important element to understand about digital citizenship is that you don't discuss it once and assume everything is good. Your institution needs to embrace and focus on your digital citizenship framework every single year. You might feel that people are getting tired of the message—and they will if your message never changes. You must review and modify your message, based on what you learned the prior year and on events in this area that need special focus. The world of digital citizenship is ever changing, so there is no reason for your message to become stagnant.

To wrap up this chapter, here are some final thoughts. Based on my experiences over the past three years, had we not focused on digital citizenship as one of our initiatives and spent time defining and communicating our framework and focus areas, I am not sure the Web 2.0 integration initiative would have survived, and I am certain our MLD program would have received much more pushback. Whether you are embarking on a digital transformation or not, digital citizenship must be a fundamental part of your district's strategy. It is incumbent on every school system to help bridge the digital divide and provide every opportunity for students to fundamentally understand what it means to live and function responsibly in a digital world.

CHAPTER 8

Bring Your Own Device Initiative

Our mobile learning strategic plan culminated in Year Three with our final initiative—the implementation of a "bring your own device" (BYOD) program at every KISD campus. BYOD is often perceived to be the silver bullet. If the students have a "device," magic will happen. However, BYOD initiatives will not be successful as stand-alone, device-driven programs. For BYOD to truly have an impact on students' engagement and learning, it must be a component of a larger strategic plan.

We recognized this in the early planning stages of our mobile strategy and, as a result, decided BYOD would be introduced in the third year, after building a a strong foundation of understanding, acceptance, and support from our stakeholders for our other initiatives.

2009–10 and 2010–11 School Years

During the first two years of our strategic plan, we worked on four areas in preparation for the BYOD implementation.

- district readiness and preparation
- technical infrastructure
- policy modification
- communication

I'm glad we planned for a Year Three implementation of BYOD because, as it turned out, we definitely needed two years to complete all the work necessary for implementation. I must say the technical infrastructure component was by far the easiest!

District Readiness and Preparation

During our first two years of the strategic plan, we conducted two readiness assessments in preparation for BYOD, one specific to technology infrastructure and one for overall readiness of our stakeholders.

The technical infrastructure readiness assessment started in Year One and focused on three areas. First, we assessed our existing wireless network to understand current design, capacity, and most important, limitations. It was critical that we understand the current environment to ensure that the operations team was designing for those parameters for BYOD implementation. Second, we assessed rates of Internet bandwidth utilization. We first measured in Year One in order to establish a baseline data set, then measured again in Year Two. We knew that our use of Web 2.0 tools and MLDs would affect bandwidth utilization, so we analyzed the data from our first two years of data and used it to help forecast the additional impact personal devices would have on utilization. The final technology assessment was of our core security and filtering systems. As with the wireless network assessment, we wanted to clearly understand capabilities and limitations of our current support systems so that as the parameters around BYOD were defined, the operations team could take the steps necessary to ensure our support systems were sufficient.

The readiness assessment of our stakeholders took place during face-to-face meetings in Year Two, second semester. In order for the BYOD initiative to be successful, it had to be viewed as a natural progression in our strategic plan and as aligned with the other initiatives. We also needed to make sure our stakeholders were at a place with their understanding and acceptance of the strategic plan that would enable them to support BYOD. So during the second semester meetings, we explained the concept of BYOD in much more detail than we had in previous meetings and used these opportunities to see what stakeholders already understood and accepted and where they were struggling. We found the information we gathered during these meetings to be invaluable and made it the foundation for building our communication strategy.

Technical Infrastructure

As we began to discuss technical infrastructure, we found that we needed to define exactly what BYOD meant for KISD. To create that definition, we needed to answer the following questions:

1. Once personal devices were on the KISD wireless network, what would they have access to?

2. How would the devices access the KISD wireless network?

3. What types of personal devices would we allow?

4. What security protocols would have to be implemented?

Once the definition was finalized, we could begin designing the parameters of our technical infrastructure that would support our definition.

When designing a BYOD wireless network, you have two options to consider.

One option is to configure the wireless network using what I call the "Starbucks" model. In this model, a public Wi-Fi network is created for each facility, and anyone with a Wi-Fi-enabled device can connect. The public Wi-Fi network is isolated and separate from your internal network, providing a means by which anyone is allowed access.

The other option is to create a wireless network requiring user authentication just like the internal network. The challenge with this design is that in a BYOD model, you have no idea of the types of devices, operating systems, or virus protection that are authenticating to the network. Because of this, the infrastructure needs to include a mobile device management (MDM) layer that acts as the traffic cop for devices connecting to the network. The MDM layer grants access based on evaluation criteria defined by the Technology Department. Every device trying to authenticate to the network is analyzed by this MDM layer and is either allowed or rejected for access.

Once I understood the configuration options for a BYOD network, the challenge was deciding which option to select. If you think about BYOD, individuals are bringing devices into your facilities to access some type of resource. The key to deciding what configuration option to select is identifying where those resources are located. If the resources are on your private network, some type of authentication process must be required for any device seeking access. If the resources are web-enabled (that is, outside your private network), then authentication is not required—all that is needed is access to the Internet.

Cost must be considered when evaluating both options. The public Wi-Fi model will be the less expensive option and will require less administrative overhead when compared to the MDM model. Most MDM software packages are based on an individual seat license that can get expensive when schools consider a BYOD model. Additionally, while the MDM layer is effective and efficient at monitoring and protecting your internal network, there is an administrative overhead component to this layer that can't be ignored.

As I began analyzing KISD's situation, a number of considerations regarding each question emerged, leading us to the answer.

Once on the KISD wireless network, what would the personal devices have access to?

- A high percentage of our instructional resources were web-enabled. This meant students in our classrooms did not need to log into our internal network in order to access these resources; all they needed was access to the Internet.

- Instructional resources that were not web-enabled were targeted for replacement as soon as a viable web-based alternative was identified.

- The district had established a nonnegotiable requirement that any new education resource being implemented in the district must be web-enabled.

- Web 2.0 tools lend themselves perfectly to a BYOD environment because all that is required is Internet access. Web 2.0 is the great equalizer when it comes to making your environment device neutral.

How would the devices obtain access to the KISD wireless network?

- Since the majority of our resources were web-enabled, and we were aggressively seeking replacements for those that weren't, we determined the necessary access for our BYOD program was going to be limited to the Internet. There would be no need for our students to have access to the KISD internal network.

What types of personal devices would we allow?

- Because we were not allowing access to our internal network, we did not need to worry about the MDM layer. Therefore, we decided our BYOD program's only stipulation about device eligibility would be that the device be Wi-Fi-enabled.

Because of all these factors, our choice for wireless network design was to implement the public Wi-Fi model at each of our campuses. Once we had decided on our BYOD wireless network model, we began the process of designing the public Wi-Fi.

Using our readiness assessment data regarding our wireless infrastructure, we knew that the number of access points at each of our facilities needed to be substantially increased. We were fortunate that all of our facilities had a wireless infrastructure already in place; however, the initial design of our wireless network was for coverage, not density. We needed to plan for not just one device per user but multiple devices per user attaching to our public Wi-Fi network at the same time. We also needed to ensure that our core networking equipment was capable of handling a segregated public network.

My strategy during the design process was to use one vendor in the initial design and then to engage two other vendors for the review. I wanted to make sure we had multiple eyes on the design, providing the checks and balances necessary to ensure our design was scalable, supportable, and cost-effective. Our philosophy was to design the public network for maximum capacity with an initial implementation at a minimum baseline. I used this approach to ensure we didn't over purchase equipment based on a utilization assumption. For this strategy to be effective, my networking department needed to have the necessary tools in place to forecast trends and utilization on the public network. I wanted expansion of our public network to be proactive, based on trends and forecasts, rather than reactive, based on help-desk tickets from our end users.

A second critical component of our BYOD infrastructure was Internet bandwidth. Once again we used the data gathered in our readiness assessment as our starting point. While this was very useful information, I didn't want it to be our only data set. We leveraged the relationships with our design vendors to get utilization data from their other customers. We did not limit the scope of data only to customers in education. BYOD was also picking up momentum in the private sector, and that data would be equally as valuable. Finally, we contacted other school districts that had implemented some type of BYOD or 1:1 model. This data set was especially valuable because those districts were also heavy users of Web 2.0 tools. With this data from multiple sources, we were able to establish some great forecasting data sets, which we plugged into our trending and forecasting tools to predict what our utilization might look like with a BYOD program.

While the forecasting data was useful from a planning perspective, it would be useless if we could not quickly expand our Internet bandwidth if utilization rates increased. As a result, we needed to ensure all our contracts allowed for bandwidth increases during the school year. Using our forecasting models and renegotiating our bandwidth supplier contracts put the Operations Department into a proactive versus reactive support model.

Following the same strategy we used with our wireless infrastructure, we planned for maximum and implemented to a minimum baseline. Using trending and forecasting models, we implemented two Internet pipes with the following bandwidths:

- Pipe A: 300 Mbps, burstable to 400 Mbps

- Pipe B: 400 Mbps, burstable to 1 Gbps

When considering the final question we needed answers for the KISD definition of BYOD to be complete, and the following considerations emerged:

What security protocols would have to be implemented?

- **Wireless utilization and trends.** The Operations Department needed monitoring tools that would allow us to track wireless utilization at all the schools. Our initial design was to create three groups from which we could track elementary, junior high, and high schools. After the first year, this proved to be not detailed enough. My recommendation would be to implement tools that would give you the ability to track wireless utilization at individual campuses.

- **Internet utilization.** We also needed the ability to track usage by specific sites. We used this site-specific data to determine the top 10 sites consuming our Internet bandwidth and to allocate bandwidth percentages to specific sites. In other words, we had the ability through our network tools to limit the amount of Internet bandwidth YouTube could use.

- **Filtering.** We needed filtering in place that accommodated the dynamic environment and nature of Web 2.0, while providing the security level necessary to ensure compliance.

It was very important to take the time to define what BYOD would look like in KISD. As you can see, deciding on the device was not the first question to be answered. As I have said many times throughout the book, it's not about the device. What drove our technical infrastructure design was the education resources and how we wanted our students to access them. The device was a result of this decision, not the driver for it.

Policy Modification

From a policy perspective, we needed to identify the usage parameters for our elementary, junior high, and high school campuses. I created a BYOD principals' committee with representation from each campus level. At our first meeting, I discussed the concept of BYOD, and I shared the readiness and preparation work that had been occurring during the previous two years. The goal for our first meeting was to give the committee a foundation from which they could formulate:

- concerns
- control parameters
- policy modifications

We subdivided the committee into elementary, junior high, and high school groups, learning from past meetings that each group had its own distinct considerations. Coming up with one-size-fits-all policies and procedures for BYOD wouldn't be realistic. I knew if we wanted to get consensus for the policy, we needed to make sure each group was viewed separately so the groups would endorse the policy changes for their particular group. If the principals felt a sense of ownership, they would work more readily with their peers and not only support the changes but defend them.

Concerns

We brought each principal group back after giving them time to consider the topics listed above. Their concerns were similar: classroom management, disruption, technical support, and parents' support. They were worried that introducing personal devices would disrupt the classroom, causing teachers to spend more time on device management than instruction.

Fortunately, we had two years' worth of experience at our MLD campuses to address these concerns. On our MLD campuses, classroom management issues didn't escalate because of our MLDs—they just looked different. For teachers using Web 2.0 tools in the classroom, their management had already changed, and introducing BYODs wouldn't be an issue. The bottom line was if the teacher just sits behind the desk, there would be classroom management issues, whether or not students used personal devices. Likewise, if the teacher is up and moving around the class, he or she can manage the students and their devices very efficiently.

Disruption and cheating, other aspects of classroom management, were next on the list of concerns. Cheating has been around since the beginning of time. If students want to cheat, they will find a way. Similarly, if students want to disrupt the class, they will find a way. These two issues are not unique to the BYOD classroom but are brought up as a potential barrier in every BYOD discussion I have had. The fact is that effective classroom management still controls the learning environment for the students. Good teachers know how to manage their classrooms to minimize disruption and cheating—BYOD has nothing to do with it.

The next concern was technical support. My response to this was somewhat tongue-in-cheek. I asked how many of the principals had asked a group of teens, "Hey, do any of you know how to <do any task> on this phone/tablet/laptop?" and not had multiple volunteers demonstrate exactly what do to. Technical support was not going to be an issue for teachers because they had a room full of young help desk analysts ready and willing to answer any question related to a device.

Control Parameters

The discussion on control parameters was very different depending on the group level. Elementary principals wanted BYOD for only Grades 2–5. They felt that prekindergarten, kindergarten, and first grade students were too young and that using devices with such young children would be a distraction and problematic for teachers. They wanted personal devices to be used only in the classroom at the teacher's direction.

Junior high principals were split down the middle. Half of the group wanted the same usage parameters as the elementary schools, and the other half wanted no usage restrictions. Since this was the first year of implementation for our BYOD program, we decided to err on the side of caution and implement the elementary usage policy for our junior highs. Personal devices could be used only in the classroom at the teacher's direction.

The high school principals were unanimous in their usage policy. They wanted unrestricted use of personal devices, which meant before school, at lunch, after school, and during passing periods between classes. Inside the classroom, personal devices could be used at the teacher's direction.

The policies that needed to be reviewed and possibly modified included:

- Responsible Use Guidelines
- Discipline Management Policy
- Student Code of Conduct
- Enrollment forms

We needed to make sure that each policy was changed to accommodate the varying usage polices for our campuses and that any verbiage restricting the use of personal electronic or cellular devices was modified in the Responsible Use Guidelines.

Our Discipline Management Policy was one document that was affected dramatically over time. As we began using the Web 2.0 tools and MLDs, when discipline issues did occur, our policy in some cases was not clear on what to do or was very prescriptive and did not allow the teachers or administrators to use the situation as a learning opportunity. We also found inconsistencies in the application of our policy from campus to campus. This started to cause problems with parents because they discovered a particular discipline infraction was handled differently depending on their child's campus. As a result, we worked very hard on our discipline management document to include the new disciplinary infractions that were occurring as a result of our initiatives and, more important, the resulting consequences for each infraction.

Modifying the policy was just the first step. We had to ensure that principals understood the chaos they were causing with the inconsistencies and that they also understood the policy changes. We wanted the principals to work with the central office when issues not clearly defined in our policy occurred (and they always do and did), so we could formulate a district response and disseminate the information about the new issue to all their peers. We added some specific verbiage related to BYOD to our policies. One of our new requirements was that when using personal devices, students must be on the KISD public wireless network. If a student was caught using their device and it was not on the KISD public network, specific disciplinary actions would result.

Communication

From the readiness assessment data gathered in the second semester of Year Two, the team had a good grasp of where the stakeholders were struggling with BYOD concepts and what needed to be addressed in the communication portion of the initiative's rollout. During our discussions with stakeholders in the previous two years, we were able to talk about long-term district goals regarding personal devices. And while we did not go into a lot of detail about BYOD in our first two years, we did do a fairly good job of helping our stakeholders understand the concept as it related to digital citizenship. We found that our digital citizenship framework and discussions naturally led to a fundamental understanding of the concept of BYOD.

What we had not done effectively is help our stakeholders understand the alignment of BYOD with our other two initiatives, mobile learning and Web 2.0 integration. This was a surprise to me. I assumed that if the stakeholders understood the concept of BYOD, they would naturally understand how all of our initiatives aligned with and supported one another. However, our stakeholder readiness data showed a disconnect between BYOD concepts and our work leading up to the implementation, particularly for teachers and parents. This disconnect was the starting point from which all our communication began. We needed the implementation of our final initiative to be viewed as an aligned, natural progression in our strategic plan, not something radical or unorthodox.

I wanted the communication strategy to focus on the fact that everything we had done for the past two years to prepare our teachers, students, and parents for the new reality of mobile learning was directly related to BYOD. Our work to integrate Web 2.0 tools into the classroom had created a learning environment that was device- and platform-neutral—allowing personal devices to become "enablers" for learning. We needed to make sure our stakeholders clearly understood how this would be possible with all devices.

As part of this, we looked back at the feedback from our teachers about our Web 2.0 integration initiative. As we talked with teachers who were using Web 2.0 tools in the classroom, we had asked them to note areas of improvement or areas of concern. The number-one answer to that question was that they wanted to increase the number of devices available to their students. The answer to their concern was, of course, BYOD! Allowing students to bring in their personal devices would definitely increase the number of devices available. Making connections such as these helped our teachers and all our stakeholders understand how BYOD was a learning enabler and how it was tightly integrated within our strategic plan.

The issue of equity was often brought up in our discussions regarding BYOD. This is one of the most important points any school system considering a BYOD implementation needs to address clearly with all its stakeholders: *BYOD does nothing to address equity issues.* Implementing BYOD allows school systems to leverage the personal technology investments parents have made in their children. This allows school systems to share some of the financial burden associated with technology with their parent community. Let me be clear, while BYOD does nothing to address equity, lack of equity is a consequence that must be confronted. We were fortunate in that every campus had a number of mobile laptop carts. Our response to the equity concern was going to be two-fold. First, with the change of instruction and through the use of Web 2.0 tools, we were seeing our teachers incorporate more project-based learning methodologies. With this type of instruction, it is feasible for students to share devices among their project teams. Second, we would make the computers in the mobile laptop carts available in a different way. Rather than checking out an entire laptop cart, teachers could check out individual laptops as supplements for those students who did not have a personal device.

With that, the foundation for our communication strategy as it related to BYOD was defined. We would focus on showing how work done in the previous two years was tightly aligned to and integrated with BYOD and how it was preparing our teachers and students for a BYOD learning environment. We would show teachers how personal devices could be used to enable learning with Web 2.0 tools and increase the number of devices available in their classrooms. BYOD was not going to solve for equity; however, we understood this and planned to leverage project-based learning models and changes in mobile laptop availability to address the issue.

Once the usage policies had been agreed on with the BYOD principal committee, I presented the BYOD and proposed usage policies to the school board, using the communication framework defined above. We began working on our BYOD policy changes toward the end of our second year, which gave us plenty of time to work with the school board and community in preparation for BYOD implementation in the 2011–12 school year.

I presented to the school board multiple times, focusing specifically on the required modifications to our administrative guidelines and usage policies. I wanted to give the board members numerous opportunities to ask questions and receive input from the community. While board members asked plenty of questions about BYOD and, in particular, the usage policy, I never once felt as if the school board was in any way opposed to or questioning our mobile philosophy or BYOD initiative. I am glad we planned enough time, so that I had the opportunity to talk to the board on multiple occasions.

When it came time for the board to approve administrative regulations and policies for the 2011–12 school year, our BYOD modifications passed with a 7–0 vote, once again signifying that our district and community understood and accepted our mobile philosophy.

Beyond spending time with the school board, we did not do a lot of communication specifically on the topic of BYOD in the year before rollout. For parents, we waited for the summer to begin our communication plan. We felt that if we started too early, the message would be lost or forgotten. Arranging face-to-face meetings during the summer was very difficult; however, we knew the message needed to get out. We used our district and campus websites to get the framework messaging introduced. For the start of school, we wanted to have material that would be sent home with all students in their first-day packets.

We created a Parent Guide for BYOD, providing parents with background on what BYOD is and why KISD was implementing it, specifying what devices could be brought to school, answering frequently asked questions, and providing digital responsibility tips and tricks. It also included an approval form for parents to sign, signifying they had reviewed the guidelines with their child and agreed to the terms. The guide proved to be a beneficial communication tool, one that I feel eliminated many calls to the campuses or my office. We also created a frequently asked questions section on our district web page and often referred parents to it if they had questions.

For our teachers, we created BYOD-specific material for our knowledgebase, as we knew this was a resource many of our teachers were accessing frequently. We also included communication framework discussions in the summer trainings we conducted for Web 2.0 tools.

2011–12 School Year

With most of the heavy lifting related to BYOD completed in the previous two years, our biggest challenge for the actual implementation was to make sure our stakeholders understood the communication framework and some logistical specifics regarding BYOD.

BYOD would be available at all of our campuses for Grades 2–12. We predicted that classrooms where the teachers were already using Web 2.0 tools would have the greatest success in leveraging personal devices as enablers in the instructional process. However, it was our hope that the increased number of devices would kick-start the adoption rate of Web 2.0 tools. Additionally, with students bringing in devices, we felt those teachers who had yet to adopt the Web 2.0 tools would feel pressure to try them. This might give them the incentive they needed to get on board with Web 2.0 integration.

For the 2011–12 school year we continued to use face-to-face meetings to get out our message. Awareness of the implementation of BYOD had penetrated a large portion of our parent community during the summer and, as a result, was the primary topic of conversation at these meetings during the first months of school. I'm glad we took time to analyze the readiness data because our communication framework addressed virtually all the concerns introduced at the meetings. However, we missed one important concern that will be discussed in the Reflections section.

Implementation Strategy

Our strategy for implementation was to focus on campus-level leadership. We took advantage of the administrative training session that occurs with campus leadership right before the start of school to discuss the upcoming BYOD implementation. The good news was that this was not something new to them. The principals that were on the usage policy committee had done a thorough job of letting their peers know BYOD was coming and how they arrived at the usage policy decision. We also wanted to make sure principals understood why BYOD was being implemented.

We talked about BYOD alignment with our strategic plan by using the communication framework. One of the key points we wanted principals to understand was our policy on students using KISD's public wireless network when using their personal devices and the disciplinary consequences of not following the policy. The majority of our principals embraced this initiative, although there were some who were skeptical about students bringing their devices and would require more conversations to convince. These meetings were a productive start to implementing BYOD at the campus level.

Going into Year Three, every campus had a well-established group of teachers who were frequently using Web 2.0 technology. We decided to focus on this group for initial adoption of BYOD in the class-room. The challenge was, due to the reduction of our Instructional Technology Team, these teachers would have to be helped instead by the instructional coaches assigned to each campus. Our Instructional Technology Team would need to dedicate time to the instructional coaches to ensure they understood BYOD and how teachers could leverage it for learning. One of the main methods for reaching as many of these Web 2.0 teachers as possible to talk about BYOD and related issues was conducting webinars early in the year.

Previously in this book, I talked about letting adoption grow organically within an organization. The implementation of our fourth initiative was the perfect example of that strategy. We focused on the user group who would benefit the most from BYOD, campus leadership in this case, to start the adoption process. We removed possible barriers to adoption. We ensured that the technology infrastructure was reliable and sufficient. In addition, we provided the necessary teacher support and professional development opportunities.

BYOD Reflections

As I reflected on the first year of BYOD, I focused on four key implementation areas from which overall success or failure could be determined.

- technical infrastructure
- policy modification
- communication framework
- stakeholder adoption

Technical Infrastructure

The design of KISD's public wireless network was successful. The strategy of designing for maximum utilization and implementing to a minimum baseline proved to be advantageous. In the first year, we didn't come close to reaching our maximum utilization, so had we implemented for maximum use, we would have ended up with a lot of unnecessary equipment and expense. We were pleased to see when we evaluated our actual utilization rates, that our trending and forecasting models had been quite accurate.

Our operations team had some challenges with management of the two wireless networks in the beginning. We had brought in consultants in a number of areas during the implementation of our public network, and the crosstraining that occurred between the consultants and KISD employees turned out to be inadequate. As a result, some issues arose that my staff was ill-equipped to handle. However, through further training, we were able to resolve these issues by the time we left for winter break.

Our Internet bandwidth utilization continued to grow throughout the year as BYOD adoption increased. Our forecasts and trending expectations again closely aligned to actual results. We were able to use a network management tool to allocate percentages of our Internet pipe to certain websites. Once we put bandwidth limitations on YouTube, our highest bandwith consumer, capacity was not an issue.

We found that we needed more specificity on our usage reporting. Because we were using one SSID pass phrase for the entire public wireless system, there wasn't an easy way for us to get detailed reporting by campus. We planned for future design changes to improve our ability to generate campus-specific usage reports.

We also needed to shrink the time frame for replacing our internally locked resources with web-enabled applications. While our BYOD penetration was outstanding that first year (77%), particularly at the secondary level, lack of access to critical instructional resources remained a real barrier to districtwide usage of BYOD.

Policy Modification

The usage policy developed by our principal committee was well supported by campus staff and parents. In fact, the high school principals said the change was the best thing that had occurred at their campuses in many years. Because the issues of policing cell phones usage had been removed, along with the associated administrative overhead, the overall climate of our high school campuses seemed greatly improved. The policy was so successful at our high schools that junior high principals unanimously recommended the same usage rules be applied to their campuses.

Communication Framework

I believe our communication framework helped us to accomplish the goal of communicating the integration and alignment of our BYOD initiative with the other three initiatives. This success was proved by the fact that in our first year rolling out BYOD, I received *fewer than five calls* from stakeholders (parents, teachers, administrators, and board members). Even during this first year, enough teachers were taking advantage of BYOD that there would have been more calls to my office if the communication framework had not been successful.

The one area we had left out of our framework was student safety. Looking back, I am not sure how we missed this initially because this concern came up in every one of our MLD parent night meetings. However, we quickly incorporated into our BYOD presentations how we were addressing student safety as it related to personal devices. Parents' biggest concern was students' access to inappropriate content as well as others' access to their children's personal data.

Their concern about access to inappropriate content at this point was a little surprising. This should have been voiced long before we started talking about BYOD in KISD. Nevertheless, we used this as another opportunity to educate our parent community on digital citizenship. We explained to them that we had created a public wireless network their children would connect to while in school and that this network had the same level of age-appropriate filtering as our desktops. However, when their children connected to their home wireless network or any other public wireless network, there would be no filtering, and they could get to any website. It was really interesting to see how many parents had no clue about this very basic concept of wireless networks.

Stakeholder Adoption

Our lowest BYOD utilization was at the elementary level, which was no surprise to me. Among elementary classrooms, utilization was highest for our fourth and fifth grade students and quickly tapered off for younger students. I don't believe this reflects anything other than parental apprehension over sending devices to school with young students. I can fully appreciate that feeling—my son is on his third iPhone and is a senior! Adoption was highest at our high schools. In our junior highs, adoption was dependent on the number of teachers utilizing the Web 2.0 tools.

Looking at individual stakeholder groups, let's start with the easiest stakeholder group, students. Adoption was immediate from the first day of school, period, end of story!

Adoption by parents was based on the pressure they were receiving from their children to bring a device to school. This was not a bad thing and was an intended outcome from our communication framework.

Adoption by principals was where we saw the greatest variation at every level. It was clear from talking to students in the first year of BYOD which principals were embracing this initiative and which principals were simply complying. I was expecting to see this variation at the elementary level because parents had more influence on whether devices came to school compared to the secondary level. However, at the secondary level, if you saw students at lunch on their devices or in the library using their devices, you knew this was a campus where the principal was truly embracing BYOD and making it part of the campus culture. It was disappointing to go to a campus, particularly a high school campus, and see no fundamental difference from the previous year. On the bright side, BYOD was still being used in individual classrooms on these campuses, but it was not becoming part of the campus culture, and students were still frustrated.

As expected, BYOD adoption was highest with our teachers utilizing the Web 2.0 tools. We were expecting the introduction of BYOD would help increase the Web 2.0 adoption for the third year. To our surprise, we did not see a dramatic increase in the number of new teachers adopting Web 2.0 tools compared to the second year. My personal belief is that the primary reason for this was the reduction in staff within our Instructional Technology Team. When we had a dedicated team whose sole focus was the implementation of our initiatives, adoption significantly increased, as was the case between Years One and Two. Though this reduction was necessary for other reasons, it meant that we did not see a significant adoption increase. However, teacher tech support was *not* an issue.

Toward the end of the first year using BYODs, we surveyed our secondary students and teachers to measure device utilization. Roughly 80% of our students responded. The response rate for teachers was fairly low (1,606 teachers out of approximately 4,000— approximately 40%) but still statistically significant and valuable to us.

Secondary Student Survey Results

Do you bring your own device to school?

> Yes (77%)
>
> No (23%)

What device do you bring?

> smartphone (54%)
>
> iPad (41%)
>
> other (5%)

Do you have at least one computer or device to use at home?

> Yes (98%)
>
> No (2%)

Do you have Internet access at home?

> Yes (98%)
>
> No (2%)

Teacher Results

Do you bring your own device to school?

> Yes (38%)
>
> No (62%)

Do you incorporate BYOD into your instruction?

> Yes (33%)
>
> No (67%)

What would make you more likely to use BYOD more frequently in your classroom?

> More supplemental devices (46%)
>
> Ideas on how to incorporate BYOD (21%)

How often do you get requests to help students with hardware problems on their devices in class?

> Daily (4%)
>
> A few times a month (10%)
>
> Rarely (20%)
>
> Never (25%)

A couple of findings jumped out at me as I analyzed the survey results.

First, the reported number of students bringing their own devices did not seem to support the teacher response of needing more supplemental devices. Although we needed to examine this statistic in more depth, I strongly suspected teachers were not recognizing smartphones as devices capable of performing the functions they required in their classroom. Smartphones can provide these functions, based on what we have seen for three years with our MLD program; nonetheless, if half of our responding secondary teachers felt this way, it was something we needed to address. In subsequent training and modeling sessions, we made sure to emphasize that devices should not be limited to laptop or tablet models and that smartphones were viable tools that could successfully be incorporated into instruction.

Additionally, we created webinar sessions between our MLD teachers and secondary teachers providing opportunities for collaboration on instructional opportunities using smartphones.

The second thing that I realized is that, while Web 2.0 integration had been occurring in the district for two years, we still had a small subset of teachers (21%) who said they needed more ideas on how to incorporate BYOD. This might mean that these teachers were still instructing in the traditional model, not using Web 2.0 tools, and with this limited experience unaware of how personal devices could be used. This would be a discouraging possibility, given that we were three years into our strategic plan. The more positive possibility was they just didn't understand how BYOD and Web 2.0 integrated and supported each other. Either way, we needed to identify this subset of teachers and determine the corrective course of action. The challenge was identifying where these teachers were located in our district.

To close this chapter out, I claim the first year of BYOD as a success, given the results in each of the key implementation areas: technical infrastructure, policy modification, communication framework, and stakeholder adoption. Beyond the implementation, the first year of BYOD also validated our community's understanding and support of our mobile learning philosophy.

PART THREE

Future Plans and Conclusion

In Chapter 9, I take each initiative and outline the plans we put in place for the fourth year on our mobile journey. In Chapter 10, I share my closing thoughts about KISD's journey and mobile learning in general.

What's Next?

The end of the three-year strategic plan didn't mean the end of the strategic goal or the initiatives. As we began planning for the 2012–13 school year, we found we still had plenty of work to do. The mobile learning initiative needed changes due to a cut in grant funding. For our Web 2.0 integration and BYOD initiatives, we still needed to increase the adoption rates. Addressing cyberbullying issues and keeping our libraries relevant in the digital age were identified as focus points for the next year of the digital citizenship initiative.

Mobile Learning Initiative

We prepared for the 2012–13 school year under the assumption that no federal funding for our mobile learning device (MLD) program would be available, which was wise, as an additional FCC "Learning on-the-Go" grant was denied. If you recall, in our second year of the initiative, we rolled out the MLD program to fifth grade classes at 11 elementary campuses and funded that program 100 percent from the KISD general operating fund. The third year, we expanded to seven additional campuses, keeping the KISD MLD budget the same and using the grant money to fund the expansion.

When we decided to expand to the seven additional campuses, I made it clear to the superintendent's cabinet that should that funding disappear, our existing MLD budget could not cover the data plans for the additional campuses. However, the devices could still be used on our public wireless network and, as such, would still have educational value. The consensus from the cabinet was to move forward with the expansion and keep MLDs at all 18 campuses.

With the grant funding denied, seven of our MLD campuses would not have data plans associated with their devices beginning the 2012–13 school year. To determine which campuses would not have data plans, we used survey and observational data to rate all MLD campuses for breadth and depth of use, as well as academic performance. The lowest-rated seven campuses would not have data plans for the upcoming school year.

On the positive side, Verizon presented an opportunity for us to upgrade, free of charge, our MLDs that were two years old. Given that the life cycles of these devices are much shorter than a typical classroom hardware device, we jumped on the opportunity. The upgrade program allowed KISD to swap out approximately 1,200 devices. The icing on the cake for us was that Verizon let us keep the two-year-old devices. We now had 1,200 additional Wi-Fi-enabled devices that could be used in some form or fashion in our classrooms.

The challenge for deploying the extra MLDs was that these devices were truly disposable—if and when they broke, they would not be replaced. I hate introducing a program that has a short life cycle and no plan for sustainability. However, I didn't want to turn up my nose at 1,200 extra MLDs. One option was to offer these devices to additional elementary campuses. However, since one of our goals was to increase the number of teachers and students using BYOD, I instead decided to leverage the MLDs to increase BYOD adoption. Based on the data from the first year of our BYOD program implementation, I determined this could best be accomplished by deploying the MLDs at the junior high level.

I offered the devices to principals at the three junior high schools with the highest number of students receiving free and reduced-price lunches. All three of the principals felt these devices would be of great value, not only for the students, but also for teachers as they worked to integrate BYOD into their classrooms. The MLDs could be used to address equity issues that would be more likely at these campuses. We determined that each junior high would receive roughly 400 MLDs, with the understanding that when they broke, there would be no replacements.

The principals at the three schools were great instructional leaders and leveraged these devices at every opportunity. Just like at our elementary campuses, each of the junior highs had teachers who immediately incorporated the devices into their instruction. Some of the junior high campuses used the devices in a "class set" model, creating a 1:1 model that was very successful. This was beneficial because it showed teachers who were struggling to adopt BYOD how this type of device could be used as an enabler for instruction. Some of the devices were allocated to the library and could be used there by students to conduct research or do homework. The bottom line is these principals took the MLDs and made them a critical component of their instructional process.

Web 2.0 Integration and BYOD Initiatives

Our Instructional Technology Team was facing a unique situation in the fourth year. This was the first time in three years members were not responsible for introducing anything new related to the strategic plan. We wanted to leverage this new bank of time wisely by focusing specifically on teachers who were struggling to incorporate Web 2.0 tools or BYOD into their classrooms. We planned to offer more face-to-face instruction and more webinars, providing opportunities for teachers in specific grades or teaching the same subject to collaborate. For example, at webinars where ninth grade science teachers could get together online and discuss upcoming lessons and how Web 2.0 tools or BYOD could be incorporated.

In addition to providing help with instruction, it was important to identify the subset of teachers who had yet to use Web 2.0 tools or BYOD and to understand their barriers to adoption. In a perfect world, this process would have been the responsibility of campus leadership; my department should not be taking on this task. But since this wasn't our situation, we also needed to look at our campus leadership and understand what they were and were not doing to increase adoption.

Improving Data Analysis

When I met with the Instructional Technology Team to discuss our goals for the 2012–13 year, we struggled with exactly how we could improve adoption rates of Web 2.0 tools and BYOD throughout the district. We didn't have an accurate count of how many campuses and classrooms were now using Web 2.0 tools and BYOD, making it difficult to define a growth plan. Since we didn't know our starting point, how could we measure improvement? Also, because the Instructional Technology Team was down to four staff members, we couldn't send them out to every campus to analyze the campus culture and identify the barriers to adoption. We knew the barriers were either at the campus level or the individual classroom teacher level. The key was identifying the data sets that would help identify which of the two barriers existed.

Beyond identifying the data required, we had to find out if the data existed, where it existed, how we would extract it, and how often it would be reviewed. Once the campus data had been identified and analyzed, we could identify targeted strategies to improve adoption. We knew going into the school year we would not overcome all barriers at every campus; however, we did want to make a dent.

To find data to help us understand the principals' role in enabling adoption, we looked to our area superintendents, the group of leaders in KISD that the principals reported to. We wanted to use the data they were collecting to evaluate the principals as our starting point. Unfortunately, we discovered that this was an area that had not been integrated thoroughly into our strategic plan. The evaluation criteria for principals had not been modified to include leadership measurements related to our strategic plan. From this we learned that it is *very important* when embarking on this type of change, to look at all areas of your organization and how the strategic plan could affect each, including the individual evaluation criteria specific to your plan. Had we done this from the beginning of our implementation in the first year, we could have leveraged this data to see where we had leadership issues and identified the specific areas of leadership that needed to be addressed. But due to the lack of hard data, we were forced to use subjective information from our area superintendents and Instructional Technology Team.

To help us identify those teachers who were struggling with adoption, we turned to the power users of Web 2.0 at each campus to help us. The key to getting input from them was making them comfortable with identifying these teachers. Their first reaction to this question was usually, "I'm not going to get any teacher in trouble," which is completely understandable. We made sure that the power users understood our intent, that we wanted to provide additional support to these teachers and no negative repercussions were going to result. Once they understood this, we were able to identify a number of teachers at each campus who were still struggling with adoption.

We also needed an analytical tool that could help the Instructional Technology Team measure technology use. We hoped this could be used as a prescriptive tool that could help us increase Web 2.0 and BYOD adoption. Prior to the start of the school year, I decided to purchase an analytical tool from BrightBytes (www.brightbytes.net). This tool had a predetermined set of survey questions that campus staff members would respond to. The survey questions focused on four areas: classroom integration of technology, campus and classroom environment, teacher skills, and access. An interesting thing about this survey is how it took into consideration teachers' personal use of technology outside the classroom. When you think about it, this makes sense. If teachers didn't interact or use technology in their personal lives, chances were greater they might struggle with embracing Web 2.0 and BYOD. Based on the data provided by teachers and the algorithms, the system would produce analytics and reports for each campus. Our plan was to administer this survey at the beginning of school, use the data to determine prescriptive training and areas of focus for each campus, and then at the end of the year give the survey once again. This would allow my team as well as other departments to see where we had achieved growth and where we still had work to do.

Instructional Coaches

In addition to using our new analytical tool, we planned to work more closely with instructional coaches to ensure they had the knowledge and skills necessary to promote and support increased adoption. This would be our second year with the instructional coaching model, and they would be more settled into their new roles. As a result, we were expecting more focus on technology integration for our fourth year.

To measure how much our instructional coaches were affecting adoption, we would use the BrightBytes reports on teacher technology use, broken down by campus. As the instructional coaches would be responsible for turning the results of the beginning-of-year survey into prescriptive training, we could use the result of our end-of-year survey to measure how effectively the instructional coaches were influencing adoption.

Improving Laptop Use

One thing we heard consistently from principals and teachers in the first year of BYOD implementation was how they would like to use laptops as supplemental devices, but they took too long to boot up. If three quarters of the class is up and running with personal devices, and one quarter of the class is waiting on a district laptop to boot up, this is not a good scenario.

We traced the problem to the fact that students had to log in to their laptops with their own IDs. The creation of these unique profiles slowed the login time. If the teachers are using Web 2.0 tools and some of their students are bringing in their own devices, there is no reason why students would need to have individual IDs. So over the summer, we would create generic IDs for each campus that could be used on the laptops in a BYOD classroom. By eliminating the individual login process we knew the laptop boot-up time would be decreased significantly.

Greater Broadband Access

On a technical infrastructure level specifically related to BYOD, based on our trending and forecasting data, we needed to increase our district bandwidth to:

- Pipe A: 300 Mbps, burstable to 400 Mbps

- Pipe B: 700 Mbps, burstable to 1 Gbps

We also began working with local vendors to address pockets of our district where broadband Internet access at home doesn't exist. We are fortunate at KISD—this number is relatively low. However, it is a problem we need to help solve. Broadband access at home is critical for our students. I believe it is a community problem, and we all must participate in the solution. While we are in the very early stages of BYOD, I hope that we will see public Wi-Fi at an increasing number of places, including some of our local restaurants and apartment complexes.

Digital Citizenship Initiative

Our digital citizenship objective for the 2012–13 year would again focus on cyberbullying prevention and social networking etiquette. Cyberbullying continues to be a national issue, one to which all K–12 institutions need to allocate instructional time. We planned to create videos to address this important issue and bring in guest speakers to help get out the message. I also planned to create a social networking etiquette video series for our students and parents. The intent was to create three or four videos explaining social networking, basic do's and don'ts.

Examples of cyberbullying prevention information and social networking etiquette resources we planned to use can be found in Appendix B, "Digital Citizenship Resources."

Additional Initiatives

In addition to the four original mobile learning initiatives, our Technology Department was going to focus on other areas directly linked with instruction.

Library

During the fourth year, we planned to focus heavily on the library media specialists to help them understand and embrace their new role in the migration to a digital environment. There were a number of them who were still struggling with the change from librarian to library media specialist. We planned to use the same processes that were successful with our other stakeholder groups to move them from understanding to acceptance of our strategic plan and their important place in it.

Additionally, I wanted to start redefining how our libraries were being viewed and how they functioned. For example, I wanted to change the name from "library" to "learning commons." The learning commons would be a place for students to gather and collaborate as well as to read and research. It would have movable furniture, common areas, and areas where students would have access to tablets, netbooks, gaming stations, and interactive whiteboards. Our library management system already had the ability to accommodate ebooks, and we made a significant investment in this area. Students would be able to check out library books with their e-readers and other devices. The library media specialist would be seen as a valuable resource for the students as they engage in new digital modes of inquiry and research. We planned on piloting this concept at an elementary school, a junior high, and a high school.

To make this happen, library media specialists have to be knowledgeable about digital citizenship and Web 2.0 tools. Students entering the learning commons with their personal devices would need instruction in using the tools responsibly, and how to properly conduct research and analysis using the Web 2.0 tools. This is something we would have to pace carefully because it is a new concept, and in some cases, very threatening to the traditional librarian model. However, we need to recognize that the way students access information and conduct research is very different today.

Tablets

We noticed in the previous school year that tablet computers were starting to get a lot of attention throughout the school system, and, as a result, my department was seeing a significant increase in requests for these devices from the campuses. In order for campuses to purchase tablets, the devices would have to be added to our district classroom standards list. But before they could be added, we wanted to make sure that everyone understood all the issues related to tablets, that the tablets were integrated with the direction our district was heading, and that the tablets actually added value. In order to do this, we planned to conduct a pilot program. We would pilot two tablet models at five of our elementary campuses for all grade levels. One campus would pilot the Apple iPad, and our four other campuses would pilot an Android tablet. All of the pilot projects would be using our public wireless network rather than our internal private network, so, in effect, these tablets would just be BYODs purchased by the district.

I wanted to pilot with both the Android and Apple tablets so as not to show favoritism. If they are attaching to KISD's public wireless network, it shouldn't matter what device it is. The goal for each pilot would be to define the support model required for each platform. The caveat for tablets is that there would have to be more campus-based support and administration than there is for the traditional laptop or netbook model. I wanted the campuses to understand and accept this model completely before they began using their campus budgets to purchase these devices.

The plan was for the pilot to run through the first semester. Then we would create the support and management guidelines for campuses and include these devices on our standards list for the second semester.

Moving On

This is the point in the chapter where I usually reflect on the actions taken to determine if they were effective and identify any lessons learned. However, in November of 2012, I accepted a position with the Houston Independent School District as its chief technology information officer. While this was a very difficult decision, I felt I was leaving KISD in a good place. All the items identified in our planning process for the fourth year were implemented as planned prior to my departure. But more important, the strategic plan and initiatives would continue to facilitate the philosophical change in instruction whether I was there or not. KISD was well on its way toward achieving its strategic goal of changing how teachers teach.

CHAPTER 10

Conclusion

We are experiencing the most transformational time that K–12 education has seen in decades. At the heart of this transformation is a philosophical change in the way we deliver instruction. We are recognizing that it is time we start incorporating the tools students use every day in their personal lives into the classroom. It's not about what device students are using; it's about changing instruction so that their devices enable learning to occur in a manner they are growing up with.

As district and state leaders, we must not miss this opportunity to change the traditional educational model. Using their personal technologies will allow students to demonstrate their mastery and their depth of understanding of the curriculum in ways standardized tests could never measure. Allowing students to use the tools they use in their daily lives in a nurturing learning atmosphere will materially improve their preparation for their futures. What can we do as technology leaders, instructional leaders, and community leaders to help in this philosophical change?

Transformation means a change in form, appearance, nature, or character. If you think about public education and the challenges we are trying to address, when it comes to the learning environment our students expect, it is the embodiment of transformation. We must change the form of our instruction, the appearance of our classrooms and resources, the nature of educational time constraints, and, finally, the character of that traditional education model. We must move from the mentality of *technology solution* to the mentality of *classroom experience*. Technology can no longer be considered a commodity or luxury in our classrooms or educational process.

To succeed during times of transformation, it takes leadership, commitment, and a degree of risk taking. You may to choose to lead the transformation in your system. The problem with leading is that undoubtedly there will be failures along the way—that is just part of the risk taking. However, if you are committed and have the support of all your stakeholders, when the failures do occur, you address them and move on; you don't abandon the transformation. It is a bumpy process, but at the end of the day, you and your stakeholders will have blazed the trail of transformation others will follow, and your organization will see great benefits. You may be forced to follow if you can't build the support you need from your stakeholder groups. You will be able to see what works for others and take advantage of their experiences, but you may find it impossible to catch up with them.

Whether you are leading or following the transformation, you must do something. I started this book with a chapter titled "It's Not If, It's When," and the when is now. Our students are expecting their educational experience to prepare them for their lives as adults. You must ask yourself: "What am I doing in my system to prepare them?"

It doesn't matter if you are in the consideration process or if you are in the middle of implementing a mobile strategy—I hope my road map and lessons learned are in some way beneficial. This mobile learning wheel has already been invented, not only by KISD but by many other school systems—please don't reinvent the same wheel. Take our lessons and benefit from them to make your plan or implementation even more successful.

Foundation for Success

In January 2013, I started working for the Houston Independent School District (HISD), the nation's seventh largest school district, as its chief technology information officer (CTIO). HISD wanted to begin its digital transformation journey and I was excited to be once again involved in defining the strategic plan.

I used the processes outlined in this book to define the goals, strategy, and associated initiatives for HISD. While its device solution is a 1:1 model, not BYOD, the other initiatives discussed in the book are being implemented in HISD with great success.

I have been fortunate in my career in education to lead BYOD and 1:1 initiatives for two separate school systems. While there are significant differences in each approach, my experience implementing these programs has uncovered three common areas that can determine success or failure.

Strategic Alignment. These programs are not about the device—they are about philosophically changing the way instruction is delivered. In order for this philosophical change of instruction to occur, it must be both a district and a community initiative with heavy involvement from campus leadership and the Curriculum, Technology, and Professional Development Departments. Their involvement must be from the very beginning. This will help assure alignment among the three areas at every step along the implementation path. The need for alignment does not diminish once the program is implemented—it must remain intact for as long as the program exists in your system.

Leadership. Leadership begins with the school board and extends down throughout the organization. You must spend time helping your stakeholders understand *why* you are doing this. Only after they understand the *why,* can they even begin to comprehend the *how.* Oftentimes, leadership for these types of programs is left to the "central office." However, leadership must occur at the campus level and with your parent community. Changing instruction will not be easy; you are attempting to change an education model that has been in existence for many years. Without the understanding and support of your campus leadership and acceptance from parents, adoption will be spotty at best. Most important, without understanding and acceptance in place, when bumps occur (and they will!), program abandonment will be an easy out.

Expectation Management. At its core, instructional delivery is the culture of an educational system. So when you attempt to change instructional delivery, you must also face the challenge of changing the culture. Change of this type becomes personal for your key stakeholders—teachers. You must be realistic about the adoption cycles. You will never have 100% adoption in the first year, and forcing this type of change on your teachers is a recipe for failure. When you embark on changing the instructional delivery model, remember the three groups teachers fall into: early adopters, testers, and resisters (see Chapter 5). The early adopters, although the smallest group, are your most influential. Focus on them the first year, and then leverage their ability to influence the other two groups. Don't force testers and resisters into immediate adoption, or they will push back and could even derail your program. If you take this realistic approach and use the people with the most influence to your advantage, your tester and resistor numbers will decrease with each passing year.

If you manage these three areas effectively, whether you are in the planning phase or the implementation phase, you are well on your way to success!

Do's and Don'ts

To close out this book, I offer some do's and don'ts that your leadership team should consider as you embark on this journey:

Do

- Champion the integration of technology.

- Model technology integration. If your staff members see you using technology and benefiting from it, selling integration to them becomes much easier.

- Talk with your peers. Leverage the great things happening at one campus by communicating the results to the rest of the district.

- Take advantage of virtual technologies to quickly get people together to share and learn from one another.

- Use competition as a motivator. If you showcase one campus in front of the other campuses, I guarantee you others will want to share!

- Communicate about and promote technology integration with parents.

- Ensure training and support are adequate for your staff.

- Communicate the training opportunities and monitor attendance. It's easy for individuals to say, "I don't understand" if they never attend the training. Forcing individual accountability onto your staff takes the opportunity for weak excuses off the table.

Don't

- Assume because you commanded "integrate technology" that it will happen.

- Let frustration build with your teachers because of a lack of training or understanding. Get out, observe, talk, and lead the integration process.

- Keep issues to yourself. Talk with your peers and other support staff. Remember, this is a district initiative; lean on support personnel from your central office.

- Be afraid of technology.

I have used the road map outlined in this book to successfully implement two digital transformation initiatives. While I don't believe this road map is the only way, it has a proven track record of success.

Learning together is the new normal: learn it, love it, live it! As they say in the cartoons, "That's all, folks!" I wish you the best of luck in your mobile learning journey and invite you to contact me if I can assist you on your way.

Mobile Device Applications by Content Area

The following content-specific MLD applications are the most popular currently being used in KISD. Included are apps and widgets for language arts, science, social studies, and a couple of apps for reference material. All product descriptions are provided by the app publishers.

Applications for math are not included because of the vast number of available options; this is one area where tool availability is not in short supply. Any search for math apps will result in an extensive list.

Language Arts

Dropwords

 Dropwords is a word-finding puzzle that combines some elements of Scrabble and Boggle, with a dash of Bejeweled. Valid words boost your score and the dwindling timer; used letters disappear, and new ones drop down from above.

WordSearch Unlimited

Search for words. Word lists include animals, food and drink, fruit and vegetable, family, body parts, colors, sports, transport, music and instruments, German/French/Spanish/Italian words.

Wordoid!

Use your linguistic skills to find words on the letter grid in this addictive and challenging spelling game!

Johnny Grammar Word Challenge

Beat the clock and answer as many spelling, vocabulary, and grammar questions as you can in this 60-second quiz! Johnny Grammar's Word Challenge is a quiz for English learners to test common vocabulary, spelling, and grammar that appear in everyday English.

OverDrive Media Console:
Library eBooks & Audiobooks

Read eBooks and listen to audiobooks from your library using OverDrive Media Console. More than 22,000 libraries worldwide offer titles via OverDrive.

Science

Google SkyMap

Google SkyMap turns your Android-powered mobile phone into a window on the night sky.

Google Earth

Use Google Earth to fly around the planet with the swipe of a finger. Search by voice for cities, places, and businesses. Browse layers, including roads, borders, places, photos, and more.

Metal Detector

This app is a tool to measure magnetic field values using the magnetic sensor that is built into the phone.

Sound Meter

The Sound Meter app uses your device's microphone to measure noise volume in decibels (dB) and shows a reference SPL (sound pressure level) noise meter.

Smart Measure

This rangefinder (telemeter) measures the distance, height, width, and area of a target with your phone by trigonometry. Usage is simple: just stand up and press the shutter. The important point is aiming the camera at the ground, not the object (i.e., in order to measure the distance from someone, aim at his shoes).

Moon Phase Widgets

Moon Phase Widgets displays the current phase of the moon depending on your location. View the moon daily for one month or more.

Nature Facts

This app contains thousands of nature-related facts. (animals, astronomy, biology, bugs, earth, oceans, human body, trees, weather). Available through AndroidFreeware.net.

Social Studies

50 States

Learn the states, capitals, and much, much more. For each state you will also learn the population, flag, largest city, motto, state bird, area, and highest point! Test yourself with quiz mode. The clickable map makes it easy to look up a state.

We the People

Carry United States' historical texts in your pocket.

1.3.0: Amendments 11–27

1.2.0: Constitution

1.1.1: High Contrast Text

1.1.0: Declaration of Independence

1.0.0: Bill of Rights

State Capitals

Animated cards and intuitive touch gestures help you learn all 50 U.S. State capitals in no time at all!

- Once you learn a state, mark it as known
- Shuffle the cards or sort alphabetically
- Show state name or capital name on top
- Always remembers where you left off

U.S. Presidents Facts!

Learn about our U.S. presidents with this app! From George Washington to Barack Obama, you'll learn about their birthplaces, religions, political parties, years in office, and vice presidents.

References

Dictionary.com Dictionary and Thesaurus

This reference and dictionary app delivers trusted content from Dictionary.com and Thesaurus.com. The app also features a home screen widget, voice search, audio pronunciation, and Dictionary.com's popular Word of the Day and Hot Word blog.

WikiMobile (Wikipedia Browser)

Being a walking encyclopedia is now at your fingertips. With WikiMobile, you carry 2+ million Wikipedia articles with you, including pictures.

Google Goggles

Search by taking a picture: point your mobile phone camera at a painting, a famous landmark, a barcode or QR code, a product, or a popular image. If Goggles finds it in its database, it will provide you with useful information.

Goggles can read texts in English, French, Italian, German, Spanish, Portuguese, Russian, and Turkish and translate them into other languages.

APPENDIX B

Digital Citizenship Resources

FTC Resources

The following resources are offered by the U.S. government's Federal Trade Commission (FTC; www.consumer.ftc.gov), the nation's consumer protection agency. The resources are aimed at consumers but apply to all educators using the Internet and their students.

Computer Security
www.consumer.ftc.gov/topics/computer-security
This page includes links to articles on a variety of security issues that will help you "learn how to protect your computer, your information, and your online files."

Kids' Online Safety
www.consumer.ftc.gov/topics/kids-online-safety
This page includes links to articles that can help adults talk to kids about making safe and responsible decisions online.

Living Life Online
www.consumer.ftc.gov/features/feature-0026-living-life-online
Aimed at older students, Living Life Online teaches children how to be good digital citizens: staying safe online, thinking critically, understanding advertising, and having good online and cell phone etiquette.

Social Networking Sites: Safety Tips for Tweens and Teens
www.co.brown.wi.us/i_brown/d/library/socialnetworkingsites.pdf
This PDF includes FTC facts for consumers about socializing
safely online and includes links to online safety organizations.

OnGuardOnline.gov

OnGuardOnline.gov is "a multimedia, interactive consumer education campaign launched by the FTC and a partnership of other
federal agencies and the technology industry" to help people be safe,
secure, and responsible online. This site has specialized sections for
educators, parents, and kids.

Cyberbullying
www.onguardonline.gov/articles/0028-cyberbullying
This page offers tips on preventing cyberbullying and what to
do if it occurs.

Heads Up: Stop. Think. Click. (video)
www.onguardonline.gov/media/video-0002-heads-stop-think-click
This short video for children explains that "before kids post
online, download a game or program, or buy something, they
should take a second to stop and think before they click."

Kids and Socializing Online
www.onguardonline.gov/articles/0012-kids-and-socializing-online
Tips for guiding tweens and teens as they use social networking
sites, chat rooms, virtual worlds, and blogs.

Laptop Security
www.onguardonline.gov/articles/0015-laptop-security
These are the FTC's tips for protecting laptops from theft.

Net Cetera: Chatting with Kids about Being Online (video)
www.onguardonline.gov/media/
video-0001-net-cetera-chatting-kids-about-being-online
> This video "covers what parents need to know, where to go for
> more information, and issues to raise with kids about living
> their lives online."

Net Cetera Community Outreach Toolkit
www.onguardonline.gov/features/
feature-0004-featured-net-cetera-toolkit
> The Net Cetera Community Outreach Toolkit provides several
> PDFs and a PowerPoint presentation with information on
> protecting kids online. The material can be used to give a
> community presentation or can be distributed through schools
> or PTAs.

Protect Kids Online
www.onguardonline.gov/topics/protect-kids-online
> This OnGuard Online section provides links to resources
> offering practical tips from the federal government and the
> technology industry to help parents, students, and educators
> guard against Internet fraud, secure their computers, and protect
> personal information.

Stand Up to Cyberbullying (video)
www.onguardonline.gov/media/video-0005-stand-cyberbullying
> This video for students can be downloaded as well as viewed
> online.

Stop. Think. Click: 7 Practices for Safer Computing
http://csrc.nist.gov/groups/SMA/fasp/documents/security_ate/
stopthinkclick.pdf
> This PDF is aimed at adults, covering computer security basics,
> such as identity theft, viruses, and parental controls.

Other Online Resources

Children's Online Privacy Protection Act (COPPA)
http://epic.org/privacy/kids/
>The Electronic Privacy Information Center provides information on COPPA, including top news, history, and COPPA's provisions.

Stop Cyberbullying before It Starts
www.ncpc.org/resources/files/pdf/bullying/cyberbullying.pdf
>This four-page, downloadable, PDF handout from the National Crime Prevention Council presents information on how to prevent cyberbullying.

ISTE Standards

ISTE Standards for Students (ISTE Standards•S)

All K–12 students should be prepared to meet the following standards and performance indicators.

1. **Creativity and Innovation**

    Students demonstrate creative thinking, construct knowledge, and develop innovative products and processes using technology. Students:

    a. apply existing knowledge to generate new ideas, products, or processes

    b. create original works as a means of personal or group expression

    c. use models and simulations to explore complex systems and issues

    d. identify trends and forecast possibilities

2. Communication and Collaboration

Students use digital media and environments to communicate and work collaboratively, including at a distance, to support individual learning and contribute to the learning of others. Students:

a. interact, collaborate, and publish with peers, experts, or others employing a variety of digital environments and media

b. communicate information and ideas effectively to multiple audiences using a variety of media and formats

c. develop cultural understanding and global awareness by engaging with learners of other cultures

d. contribute to project teams to produce original works or solve problems

3. Research and Information Fluency

Students apply digital tools to gather, evaluate, and use information. Students:

a. plan strategies to guide inquiry

b. locate, organize, analyze, evaluate, synthesize, and ethically use information from a variety of sources and media

c. evaluate and select information sources and digital tools based on the appropriateness to specific tasks

d. process data and report results

4. Critical Thinking, Problem Solving, and Decision Making

Students use critical-thinking skills to plan and conduct research, manage projects, solve problems, and make informed decisions using appropriate digital tools and resources. Students:

a. identify and define authentic problems and significant questions for investigation

b. plan and manage activities to develop a solution or complete a project

c. collect and analyze data to identify solutions and make informed decisions

d. use multiple processes and diverse perspectives to explore alternative solutions

5. Digital Citizenship

Students understand human, cultural, and societal issues related to technology and practice legal and ethical behavior. Students:

a. advocate and practice the safe, legal, and responsible use of information and technology

b. exhibit a positive attitude toward using technology that supports collaboration, learning, and productivity

c. demonstrate personal responsibility for lifelong learning

d. exhibit leadership for digital citizenship

6. Technology Operations and Concepts

Students demonstrate a sound understanding of technology concepts, systems, and operations. Students:

a. understand and use technology systems

b. select and use applications effectively and productively

c. troubleshoot systems and applications

d. transfer current knowledge to the learning of new technologies

© 2007 International Society for Technology in Education (ISTE), www.iste.org. All rights reserved.

ISTE Standards for Teachers (ISTE Standards•T)

All classroom teachers should be prepared to meet the following standards and performance indicators.

1. **Facilitate and Inspire Student Learning and Creativity**

    Teachers use their knowledge of subject matter, teaching and learning, and technology to facilitate experiences that advance student learning, creativity, and innovation in both face-to-face and virtual environments. Teachers:

    a. promote, support, and model creative and innovative thinking and inventiveness

    b. engage students in exploring real-world issues and solving authentic problems using digital tools and resources

    c. promote student reflection using collaborative tools to reveal and clarify students' conceptual understanding and thinking, planning, and creative processes

    d. model collaborative knowledge construction by engaging in learning with students, colleagues, and others in face-to-face and virtual environments

2. **Design and Develop Digital-Age Learning Experiences and Assessments**

    Teachers design, develop, and evaluate authentic learning experiences and assessments incorporating contemporary tools and resources to maximize content learning in context and to develop the knowledge, skills, and attitudes identified in the ISTE Standards for Students. Teachers:

    a. design or adapt relevant learning experiences that incorporate digital tools and resources to promote student learning and creativity

b. develop technology-enriched learning environments that enable all students to pursue their individual curiosities and become active participants in setting their own educational goals, managing their own learning, and assessing their own progress

c. customize and personalize learning activities to address students' diverse learning styles, working strategies, and abilities using digital tools and resources

d. provide students with multiple and varied formative and summative assessments aligned with content and technology standards and use resulting data to inform learning and teaching

3. Model Digital-Age Work and Learning

Teachers exhibit knowledge, skills, and work processes representative of an innovative professional in a global and digital society. Teachers:

a. demonstrate fluency in technology systems and the transfer of current knowledge to new technologies and situations

b. collaborate with students, peers, parents, and community members using digital tools and resources to support student success and innovation

c. communicate relevant information and ideas effectively to students, parents, and peers using a variety of digital-age media and formats

d. model and facilitate effective use of current and emerging digital tools to locate, analyze, evaluate, and use information resources to support research and learning

4. **Promote and Model Digital Citizenship and Responsibility**

   Teachers understand local and global societal issues and responsibilities in an evolving digital culture and exhibit legal and ethical behavior in their professional practices. Teachers:

   a. advocate, model, and teach safe, legal, and ethical use of digital information and technology, including respect for copyright, intellectual property, and the appropriate documentation of sources

   b. address the diverse needs of all learners by using learner-centered strategies and providing equitable access to appropriate digital tools and resources

   c. promote and model digital etiquette and responsible social interactions related to the use of technology and information

   d. develop and model cultural understanding and global awareness by engaging with colleagues and students of other cultures using digital-age communication and collaboration tools

5. **Engage in Professional Growth and Leadership**

   Teachers continuously improve their professional practice, model lifelong learning, and exhibit leadership in their school and professional community by promoting and demonstrating the effective use of digital tools and resources. Teachers:

   a. participate in local and global learning communities to explore creative applications of technology to improve student learning

   b. exhibit leadership by demonstrating a vision of technology infusion, participating in shared decision making and community building, and developing the leadership and technology skills of others

c. evaluate and reflect on current research and professional practice on a regular basis to make effective use
of existing and emerging digital tools and resources in
support of student learning

d. contribute to the effectiveness, vitality, and self-renewal
of the teaching profession and of their school and
community

ISTE Standards for Administrators (ISTE Standards•A)

All school administrators should be prepared to meet the following
standards and performance indicators.

1. Visionary Leadership

Educational Administrators inspire and lead development and
implementation of a shared vision for comprehensive integration
of technology to promote excellence and support transformation
throughout the organization. Educational Administrators:

a. inspire and facilitate among all stakeholders a shared
vision of purposeful change that maximizes use of
digital-age resources to meet and exceed learning goals,
support effective instructional practice, and maximize
performance of district and school leaders

b. engage in an ongoing process to develop, implement,
and communicate technology-infused strategic plans
aligned with a shared vision

c. advocate on local, state, and national levels for policies,
programs, and funding to support implementation of a
technology-infused vision and strategic plan

2. Digital-Age Learning Culture

Educational Administrators create, promote, and sustain a dynamic, digital-age learning culture that provides a rigorous, relevant, and engaging education for all students. Educational Administrators:

a. ensure instructional innovation focused on continuous improvement of digital-age learning

b. model and promote the frequent and effective use of technology for learning

c. provide learner-centered environments equipped with technology and learning resources to meet the individual, diverse needs of all learners

d. ensure effective practice in the study of technology and its infusion across the curriculum

e. promote and participate in local, national, and global learning communities that stimulate innovation, creativity, and digital-age collaboration

3. Excellence in Professional Practice

Educational Administrators promote an environment of professional learning and innovation that empowers educators to enhance student learning through the infusion of contemporary technologies and digital resources. Educational Administrators:

a. allocate time, resources, and access to ensure ongoing professional growth in technology fluency and integration

b. facilitate and participate in learning communities that stimulate, nurture, and support administrators, faculty, and staff in the study and use of technology

c. promote and model effective communication and collaboration among stakeholders using digital-age tools

    d. stay abreast of educational research and emerging trends regarding effective use of technology and encourage evaluation of new technologies for their potential to improve student learning

4. Systemic Improvement

Educational Administrators provide digital-age leadership and management to continuously improve the organization through the effective use of information and technology resources. Educational Administrators:

    a. lead purposeful change to maximize the achievement of learning goals through the appropriate use of technology and media-rich resources

    b. collaborate to establish metrics, collect and analyze data, interpret results, and share findings to improve staff performance and student learning

    c. recruit and retain highly competent personnel who use technology creatively and proficiently to advance academic and operational goals

    d. establish and leverage strategic partnerships to support systemic improvement

    e. establish and maintain a robust infrastructure for technology including integrated, interoperable technology systems to support management, operations, teaching, and learning

5. Digital Citizenship

Educational Administrators model and facilitate understanding of social, ethical, and legal issues and responsibilities related to an evolving digital culture. Educational Administrators:

    a. ensure equitable access to appropriate digital tools and resources to meet the needs of all learners

b.   promote, model, and establish policies for safe, legal, and ethical use of digital information and technology

c.   promote and model responsible social interactions related to the use of technology and information

d.   model and facilitate the development of a shared cultural understanding and involvement in global issues through the use of contemporary communication and collaboration tools

Index